NARROW GAUGE NEWS

GW01081478

SUMMER SPECIAL

THE BALA LAKE RAILWAY
by Patrick Ridley

Though now well established, the Bala Lake Railway can be described as a relative newcomer to the world of narrow gauge railways in Wales. Unlike others, which were built for a specific purpose over 100 years ago, the BLR only came into being in 1972 when a group of enthusiasts, under the leadership of George Barnes, acquired part of the former GWR track-bed which had extended from Ruabon to Barmouth, and which had lain derelict after the Beeching cuts of the 1960s. The chosen section ran from just south of the town of Bala, crucially on the 'wrong' side of the River Dee, 4.5 miles along the beautiful lake (the largest body of natural water in Wales) to the village of Llanuwchllyn, where the engineering and rolling stock activities were based. This location could not have been better as the old station was in a good state of repair.

The railway 'took off' very quickly, not only because it offered such a scenic trip along

The archetypal BLR scene, with Quarry Hunslet MAID MARIAN waiting to depart from the current terminus at Bala with a passenger service.

All photographs by Tim Gregson

the lake, the views being unhindered by trees and other topographical interruptions as is so often the case, particularly in the summer months, but it also quickly acquired the soubriquet of 'The Lineside Line' as there are so many excellent vantage points from which to take photographs from the lane which parallels the line for the length of the lake. Indeed, one of the many essential tasks carried out over the winter months is the annual pruning/cutting back of the foliage.

As the line was built on a standard gauge track-bed, the original ethos was not to create another traditional narrow-gauge railway, but rather to build a half-scale main line. The line's first passenger motive power was MEIRIONYDD, a diesel-hydraulic

MEIRIONYDD, the line's first passenger loco.

Built on the lines of a British Rail Western Hydraulic, with carriages bearing a passing resemblance to the then standard Mk1 carriages.

As steam locomotives from the North

One of the railway's open carriages, with a body shape loosely based on a British Rail Mark 1 coach.

Wales slate quarries became available, the motive power started to take on a more narrow-gauge feel. The first two to arrive were in the shape of a pair of ex-Dinorwic Quarry Hunslet locomotives, HOLY WAR and MAID MARIAN, ably assisted by a diesel shunter which was joined later by two others, both Ruston & Hornsby products. Over the years, other Hunslet steam locomotives have appeared, and it is worth dwelling on their remarkably disparate

The repatriated WINIFRED with a recreated Penrhyn train.

histories.

Owned for over half a century by the White brothers, the restoration of GEORGE B started in the brothers' house in South Wales but, gradually, the tasks became bigger and 'she' was brought to Llanuwchllyn where they would deal with improvements in minute detail. As the half century of ownership passed, responsibility for the completion passed to the railway's engineering team, headed by Chief Engineer, Rob Houghton, and it was a special occasion when 'she' moved under her own steam a couple of years ago. GEORGE B is now a regular item on the locomotive roster.

ALICE had been carefully retrieved from one of the upper levels in Dinorwic Quarry in a parlous state, but she was in good hands and was painstakingly restored by Alan Cliff in Llandderfel, close to Bala, after which she was purchased a few years ago by one of the BLR Directors and entered regular service on the railway. In spite of being over 100 years old, she is a regular member of the roster and provides sterling service.

The arrival of WINIFRED at the BLR could take up numerous pages but, to cut a fascinating story down the bare essentials, it is a tale of remarkable perseverance and providence.

A batch of six locomotives were put up for sale in 1966 by the Penrhyn Quarry and were purchased by an entrepreneur who sold three of them on to the Hulman Estate in Indiana, USA, which owned vast tracts of land across the state including the Indianapolis Motor Speedway where the Indianapolis 500 race is staged. Two of the locos, OGWEN and GLYDER, were hidden away in a warehouse, but WINIFRED was to be part of a special museum. However, this did not happen and she was left in a dry storage facility under the racetrack, never to move again for decades. Over the years, numerous appeals were made by interested parties about buying and repatriating this enigmatic trio but to no avail. However, after acquiring ALICE, BLR staff thought she would benefit from some more historic company, thus Julian Birley very carefully set about making and maintaining contact with the Hulman family trustees. Such was his subtle approach that after one entreaty, he was informed that the trustees would be interested in tentative discussions! Everything was distinctly delicate, as he wisely perceived that it could go wrong at any moment. Eventually, after many months of

Two more Quarry Hunslets on demonstration slate train duties - ALICE (*above*) and HOLY WAR (*below*).

HOLY WAR heads the "Barmouth Bay Express" at Llangower.

emails and phone calls, there was a green light and, after two visits to Indianapolis, a deal was struck and arrangements were made for the three locomotives to come home, WINIFRED to the BLR with the other two going to Beamish in County Durham.

The shipment by rail and sea from the USA went without a hitch, but it was on arrival in Southampton that delays occurred. The shippers simply forgot to forward WINIFRED's container, but after suitably frank discussions, arrangements were rapidly made and WINIFRED arrived 24 hours late with much fanfare at Llanuwchllyn. The container was carefully positioned and she was pulled very gently out into Welsh daylight again by ALICE.

This was in 2012 and WINIFRED was displayed at the railway. She had been remarkably well preserved during her time in storage and was almost untouched, even to the extent that the remains of her last fire at Penrhyn quarry were still in the ash-pan. Likewise, her paintwork gave a true insight into her final condition before she had left Wales. At the beginning of 2013,

the BLR Chief Engineer, Rob Houghton embarked on the lengthy overhaul, not a restoration, such was her condition, and this would last over three years, at the end of which a great day beckoned. This venerable locomotive was welcomed back into service, this time with passenger trains, on April 13th 2015, 130 years to the very day that she had been delivered, brand new, to the Penrhyn Quarry.

Over the years, there have been additions to the rolling stock as well, to supplement the normal carriages, and this is where the historic preservation theme develops. Numerous rebuilt slate wagons have arrived, to compliment the restored Hudson hoppers. The railway now has three open Penrhyn 'quarrymen's coaches' plus one of the three extant yellow 'Royal' wagons, these being built for Royal visits to quarries and which feature seats of differing inclination, so that those seated 'uphill' have squabs more angled to stop them ending up in the laps of the 'downhill' passengers on inclines! Other fascinating items have appeared, such as a Wickham Trolley plus genuine single axle trailer, a real rarity. But one piece of rolling stock which will appear one day soon is the recreation of the Penrhyn Saloon preserved in the Penrhyn Museum.

The commission for this exciting new project was initiated on the 'why not?' basis of all enterprising thoughts, and the new' coach is being built entirely by one man, David Hale, to the most exacting standards of a cabinet maker. The coach is now a bare shell, the doors have been fitted and tenders have been put out for upholstery of the highest quality, to match everything that has gone before. Having inspected this masterpiece since its inception, it is something of a tragedy that the intricate cabinet maker's art will, when completed, be mostly covered up, unseen and unappreciated by the admiring public. Even the handbrake wheel, in the style of a ship's wheel, is being fashioned from a solid piece of wood. For those interested, the BLR website (Latest News) features regular reports on the progress of this remarkable project.

Every winter, there are developments and improvements carried out on infrastructure, rolling stock and track-bed by the band of loyal and dedicated volunteers from many varied professions, who give up their free time with a smile, for the fun of achieving something worthwhile and productive. To say that their common goal is fuelled, in part, by copious amounts of tea and flapjacks, (a BLR tradition), is an understatement. But some developments need outside help, and this brings us on to two topics.

As a consequence of a generous grant from the Heritage Lottery Fund, the carriage shed has been extended by quite a margin, thus providing a lot more covered area for carriage stock and our historically important heritage wagons. The new section features three roads, one of which will eventually connect with the main line, but that is in the distant future. But the new track is set in concrete and will form part of our Interpretation Centre, where the public can view in complete safety, and sheltered from the elements, our ever increasing heritage rolling stock. Having large locking doors at each end of the long shed will be of substantial benefit too.

This aptly brings us back to the first paragraph about the current Bala terminus being on the wrong side of the River Dee. From the start of operations, passengers alight at the Bala end of the line at the former Lakeside Halt, only to find that the town is about half a mile distant. Thus it was that the Bala Lake Railway Trust was formed, under the title of the Red Dragon Project, to extend the line into down-town Bala, not an easy task. Headed by Julian Birley and ably supported by numerous volunteers, initial plans were drawn up and numerous forums, talks and presentations took place to instil the idea into Bala residents and see what they thought. To everyone's delight, and not a little surprise, there was virtually unanimous support for the project. Surveys were carried out, myriad learned opinions were sought and some very useful associates were found who could bring vital experience and knowledge to the party. Welsh politicians of all persuasions were invited to Llanuwchllyn to see what the railway was up to, not least Lord Dafydd Elis-Thomas who took the regulator of ALICE for a trip down the line in near horizontal 'liquid sunshine', to use their wonderfully positive euphemism, and who steadfastly refused an umbrella. The local council has expressed total enthusiasm for the project, agreeing with the prospectus that the extension will bring thousands more visitors every year into the town. One inspiring comment from a Welsh MP stated that "It's Bala's turn".

The plan, in brief, is to deviate from the existing Lake Halt, across the medieval bridge and then lay tracks down the middle of the modern road bridge (cyclist safety being paramount) before running behind what will be the strengthened flood wall at the eastern end of the lake, past the rugby club before arriving at a new station building near the western end of the High Street. Such is the enthusiasm of locals that a couple of shop sites near the proposed

HOLY WAR sits in the sun at Llanuwchllyn.

station have opened already, an opportunity too good to miss.

As this is written in early 2018, the station site in Bala has been acquired, the site levelled, after the dreaded asbestos problem had been eradicated, and almost every day something positive happens. But there is a long way to go, particularly with fund-raising, bearing in mind, for example, that the acquisition of a Transport & Works Order, the requirement of a piece of paper before even a sod of earth can be cut, will need a six-figure sum to be raised, hence the latest appeal. But with just three

permanent railway staff, a vast number of volunteers doing myriad tasks, plus the vital and unilateral goodwill of politicians, local people and supporters, the project will be completed. That first train will really put Bala on the map. It will make the railway, and the town of Bala, complete.

For further and more concise details of the extension project, as well as exciting appeals, please go to the specific Bala lake Railway Trust website:
http://www.balalakerailwaytrust.org.uk
The railway's website is at:
http://www.bala-lake-railway.co.uk

The stunning view across the lake, taken from the footplate.

FAIRBOURNE METAMORPHOSIS
by Graham Billington

When John Ellerton purchased the Fairbourne Railway in 1983, he had big plans in mind for the little railway, which was to be completely transformed within a two year time frame. He had already decided to replace the rolling stock and reduce the gauge to fit his Reseau Guerledan stock, but he envisaged changing the landscape at both ends of the line. Hugh Sykes was the last of the 15 inch gauge line's volunteers to leave and his camera caught the transition of the railway.

Two of the locos built for the Reaseau

Guerledan were never delivered but remained in storage. These were the first of the new stock to arrive at Fairbourne. In March 1984, DAVID CURWEN named after its builder but later to be renamed as BEDDGELERT after its prototype was to be seen behind ELAINE, a half scale replica of a Leek and Manifold loco. Later this would be rebuilt as the Fairbourne's RUSSELL. John Ellerton's first move in the reconstruction was to relay the back line inside the terminus building with a third rail, gauged at 12 ¼ inches.

On 30th September 1984, Hugh photographed the newly delivered pipes that were to be used to culvert the stream that ran through the middle of the station at Fairbourne and increase the land available for the construction of the new formation to be known as Gorsaf Newydd. Over that winter the station was to undergo a complete transformation.

In March 1985, the controversial rebuild of Guest 2-4-2 SIAN into SYDNEY having taken place the previous year, the rebuilt locomotive was photographed in the old terminus building which was now fully fitted out as the railway's workshop. Also in the picture was the other 15 inch gauge loco LILIAN WALTER, rebuilt form SYLVIA whose Daimler Magestic engine and cabs lay outside the workshop.

In the spring of 1985, the station looked totally different. The culverting of the stream had allowed the ground to be levelled over the stream bed and provide the extra land for the new track formation to be laid, initially in 15 inch gauge but capable of being brought in to 12¼ inches over the next winter.

The station building, now transformed into a state of the art workshop, was refaced alongside the new platform and a traverser installed to allow access to the new engine sheds and concrete became the new base for track laying. This would facilitate the change in gauge later in the year. A water tower was also constructed with a gantry to the engine release road, but much remained to be done with a new season looming.

Meanwhile on the other side of Beach Road, the car park of the then Harlequin Cafe was being used as a temporary storage facility for the thirty or so new carriages intended for the line. Six of these would subsequently be fitted with 15 inch gauge bogies to run in the 1985 season. More ex-Reseau Guerledan stock began to appear, goods as well as passenger. The newly built loco stabling facilities enabled the Reseau Guerledan locos, like JUBILEE (later YEO) to be prepared for their new life in Wales.

On the land behind the station steel framing went up to mark the beginning of the construction of the new carriage shed to provide covered accommodation for the rolling stock. At the same time, the old engine shed was demolished and replaced by a new build shop and ticket office fronting Beach Road. The old shop, basically a portakabin, had earlier been moved behind the workshop and refitted as a crew lodge. A new store was among other buildings to be constructed besides signal boxes located at

strategic points on the line.

At the other end of the line, a new track formation was being laid in 12 ¼ inch gauge to form a balloon loop at Barmouth Ferry, newly re-named Porth Penrhyn. This would bring the running line in on the seaward side of the peninsula and was intended to give passengers better views and make the railway more visible across the estuary from Barmouth. The first permanent railway structures were being built at the Ferry, including toilets and a cafe, but in the interim, the Reseau Guerledan canteen coach, minus bogies was located at Porth Penrhyn to provide refreshments. Fairbourne was about to get its first taste of Breton crepes after a whirlwind few months of change as a whole new era was ushered in, transforming what John Ellerton described as the greatest littlest railway in Wales.

RESTORING WWI SURVIVORS

by Cliff Thomas

The Greensand Railway Museum Trust (GRMT) was formed in 2000, initially inspired to assume ownership of Baldwin 4-6-0T WDLR No. 778 (Works No. 44656) from Amberley Museum in Sussex and restore it to working condition. GRMT officially came into existence in February 2001 and achieved registration as a charity with the Charity Commission (UK Registered Charity No. 1088460) on September 18 2001.

Thanks to a £50,000 Heritage Lottery Fund grant, donations from many people, sponsorship in kind by companies such as Alan Keef Ltd and BZ Metalcraft of Leighton Buzzard and generous support by a significant benefactor No. 778 was restored to steam in 2007, thus becoming

Greensand Railway Museum Trust's Baldwin 4-6-0T WDLR No. 778 (BLW 44656/1917) pictured in May 2016 while visiting APPEVA's Froissy-Cappy-Dompiere line on the Somme battlefield in Picardy. Now preserved, this railway was once part of the light railway systems built to serve the war effort.

Cliff Thomas

the only operational Baldwin class 10-12-D in Britain, indeed the world in as-built steam locomotive form, a distinction it retained as this was written in early 2018.

Restoring No. 778 was a massive, and very costly, task for a small Charitable Trust, whose five trustees are all past official (!) retirement age and a very long way from anyone's 'rich list'! Restorations of high-profile standard gauge steam locomotives can run up bills in the millions. In comparison, returning a roughly 12.5ton 2ft gauge loco to life for around £200,000 (£147,000 cash plus materials and work supplied cost-free in the form of sponsorship) may appear straightforward, but all things are relative, there being far fewer people and much less money around for narrow gauge projects.

Restoring No. 778 was only phase one. Steam locomotives require regular renewal of boiler certificates (conventionally every 10 years although it is not necessarily quite that simple) and overhaul. The objective is to keep this locomotive, one of a batch of 495 steam engines built in the USA by Baldwin for Britain's War Department Light Railways during World War 1 and an example known to have operated in France serving the Western Front, in operation for as long as realistically possible.

Thanks to generous donations and money earned (primarily steaming fees supplemented by a filming contract) during the locos first boiler ticket, GRMT was able to successfully see No. 778 through a rapid overhaul during the winter 2015/16 in order for it to participate in significant commemorative events marking the 100th anniversary of the Battle of the Somme during 2016 with a new 10-year ticket. In addition to running at its Leighton Buzzard Railway home (where it operates under a Management Agreement) No. 778 visited France to run on APPEVA's Froissy-Cappy-Dompiere line (a surviving section of WW1 era light railway) and Apedale Valley Light Railway for that year's major Tracks to the Trenches event.

As far back as July 14 2007, as we stood in the sun admiring WDLR No. 778 on a 'Donors Day' for those who had made its restoration possible, GRMT trustees were being asked, "what are you going to do next." At that time we had no plans other than to take a breather following the seven-year project which had brought life back to No. 778 beyond ensuring the long-term future of the iconic loco. A few years later the question had an answer.

Doubtless many assumed GRMT's follow-up project would be another steam locomotive, but the Trust was formed to undertake a project which looked as though it would not happen unless we gave it a shot, and another such situation emerged. Once again, an ex-Army locomotive, and one which is a unique survivor, we took on restoration of 40hp Armoured Simplex LR2182 built by Motor Rail and Tramcar Company of Bedford (MR461/1917).

This is not the place for a comprehensive description of the massive network of narrow-gauge railways built to supply the front-line trench systems built by both sides of the WW1 conflict across Europe. Suffice to say that standard gauge railways brought supplies up to railheads around 8-10 miles behind the front lines, from whence materials were carried forward over 60cm gauge lines. Steam locomotives, such as Baldwin No. 778, would work forward to a point where the obvious visibility of steam and smoke to enemy observers made such operation too vulnerable to shelling. Wagons arriving at such forward dumps would then continue to supply points or artillery batteries in shorter trains hauled by petrol-engined locos, often at night. In the same way that Baldwin Locomotive Works, of Philadelphia, USA, provided the preponderance of steam locomotives working these WDLR lines, the Motor Rail & Tram Car Company, of Bedford, England, provided the archetypal petrol locomotives (Tractors as they were then normally termed) employed to work the areas closest to the danger zones.

Motor Rail supplied a range of basic, but rugged and reliable, internal combustion locos to War Department Light Railways, production totalling 110 40hp Open types, 195 40hp Protected types, 34 40hp Armoured versions and 749 20hp locos – 1,088 locomotives in all. Of the 40hp design, the 'open' variety had little more than the curved body endplates, 'Protected' had additional plating including a comparatively lightweight roof while the 'Armoured' versions sported enhanced protection around the driving position and the distinctive cupola roof (noted as 'conning tower' in the original patent!). Although 34 of the armoured type seem to have been built, this total might have actually comprised 27 armoured locomotives constructed as such, plus seven 'kits' to convert open versions into armoured machines.

WDLR No. 2182 is important, being the oldest surviving Motor Rail 40hp 'Simplex' petrol locomotive built with full armour plating, the only example of its type still with its original petrol engine and the only example in the world which will present its original appearance on completion of the restoration. There is one other 40hp armoured Simplex. Also dating from 1917, this example ended up working in the Antigua sugar industry, becoming No. 8 Bessie, but has a replacement engine. A couple of years ago it was cosmetically restored in Antigua, where it remains, displaying the altered bodywork adopted when working in that country which includes the cupola roof being raised above the original mounting, thus presenting a somewhat different appearance from WW1 as-built condition.

Importantly for GRMT, No. 2182 is the perfect companion for No. 778 since they were built at close to the same time to undertake the same function, assist the allied war effort on the Western Front, with complementary roles. We have no evidence No. 2182 ever took charge of wagons hauled to a forward depot by No. 778, but this could conceivably have happened!

Delivery dates for 40hp Simplexes are somewhat confusing, but as far as GRMT is aware LR2182 was one of a batch of Armoured Tractors MR460-465 (WDLR 2181-2186) sent to France on March 24 1918. This was over a year after the indent date (Feb 14 1917) which appears on the works plates, making it difficult to be categoric. We do not have any solid information concerning 2182's Army service but photographs exist showing Nos. 2184 and 2187 on active service in France, these two apparently being completed in March 2018.

Post-WW1 it went to Richborough, Kent for disposal, was bought by Furness Brick & Tile Co Ltd of Askham Brickworks, Askham-in-Furnaces, Lancashire (now Cumbria) around July 1921 and lost its upper bodywork during ensuing industrial service which lasted until about 1963. It entered preservation in 1971, became part of the collection at (then) Narrow Gauge Railway Centre at Gloddfa Ganol (Blaenau Ffestiniog) in June 1978 and went to the Museum of Army Transport at Beverley in September 1985, initially on loan until donated to the Army by Michael Jacob on December 18 2001. While displayed at Beverley it superficially looked original, the long-gone 'armour' platework having been replicated in wood by Mr Jacob.

The Museum of Army Transport (not the same as the National Army Museum) closed in August 2003 and the Army offered LR2182 on loan to Leighton Buzzard Railway (LBR) where it arrived on March 30 2005, but seriously damaged (including destruction of the wooden cupola) by the movement contractors. The Army subsequently donated the loco to LBR but with other pressing priorities for time and money (a 2005 quotation for complete professional restoration put the cost at some £35,650) LBR was unable to progress matters. This is where GRMT stepped forward, ownership of LR2182 being officially transferred to the Trust in January 2009. LBR remains the base for LR2182 under the terms of a similar agreement to that covering No. 778.

In 2009 volunteers constructed a new replica (again, in wood) upper part to represent 2182's original appearance with the aim of boosting interest (and funds) towards full restoration. However, it proved difficult to generate finance as had successfully been done to restore No. 778 and progress was minimal until a fresh look was taken in early 2015.

GRMT decided to aim for a more basic restoration with an initial target of enabling LR2182 to move under its own power and leave construction of replacement superstructure and other non-essential details for later. Hopefully, a working

This mid-1970s picture of LR2182 at Gloddfa Ganol, Blaenau Ffestiniog, shows how its condition had deteriorated following industrial service and period in a scrapyard before entering preservation.

Chris Grimes

LR2182 (left) pictured in November 2009 with the (second) wooden upperworks constructed by volunteers to show how the locomotive originally looked. It is pictured alongside the NRM's 40hp Protected version LR3098, demonstrating the differences in the upperworks of the two types.

Cliff Thomas

chassis would stimulate interest and help raise more money to complete the project. Funding applications prepared by Trustees Terry Bendall and Tony Tomkins resulted in a PRISM fund award worth £9,053 and a £500 grant from the Museum Development - Bedfordshire Small Grants Scheme. Under the Project Leadership of Tim Ratcliffe a physical start was made. Following dismantling and shot blasting, a team of LBR/GRMT volunteers set to work on the frames at Stonehenge Works, cutting away rusted metal and replacing with new.

The original 40hp Dorman 4JO 4-cylinder petrol engine (engine No. 6209) which had not run for over 50 years was known to be seized and in poor condition. We did not know quite how poor until it was sent to Coventry Boring and Metalling Ltd for stripping and repair. Contracted work included stitch welding cracks in the cylinder block, crankcase and manifold, machining the cylinder block to accept four new liners, producing four new pistons from solid aluminium, manufacturing eight new valves and guides and a host of grinding, machining and polishing of other components.

Before and after restoration views of the 40hp Dorman 4JO 4-cylinder petrol engine (engine No. 6209) from LR2182.

Both: Tim Ratcliffe

Unfortunately, the spiralling cost did not leave any cash to contract reassembly of the engine. Mercifully, Peter Thorne undertook reassembly as a volunteer project at his home workshop. The completed engine was back at Stonehenge in late 2017 ready to be reunited with the frames.

Meanwhile, at Stonehenge Works the gearbox and clutch had received attention (the former getting a new gear and bearings), LBR members Andy Forbes and Mick Taylor re-built the radiator and 'Shop 4 Tanks' of Northampton produced, free of charge, a new fuel tank. The latter outwardly replicates in stainless steel the original tank but contains within a much smaller plastic tank to contain the petrol – cheaper to fill and more than sufficient capacity for the loco's use in preservation.

At the time this article was being prepared (spring 2018) the wheelsets were back under the frames, components were being re-fitted (including the end weights and gearbox) and the new set of drive chains were in position.

The cost of repairing the engine - it would have been easier and probably cheaper to fit a more modern engine but that would defeat the objective of restoration - set the project back both financially and timewise, defeating our ambition of LR2018 running in 2017. However, the award of a £3,300 grant by The Association of Industrial Archaeology (AIA) to finance replication of the distinctive cupola roof to restore its original appearance has altered, much for the better, the scope of the project.

The steelwork, primarily the cupola but also the side doors, will be fabricated and assembled by a contractor and current thinking is to have this done on their premises rather than discover any fitting issues after plates have been delivered to the restoration site. In turn, it is far easier to complete the remaining work on the mechanical components without the 'bodywork' in position. So, we anticipate finishing the chassis, including plumbing, wiring and control linkages with the consequent red letter day when the restored engine is started for the first time, at Stonehenge

This August 31 2009 picture shows GRMT's two locomotives alongside each other, for various reasons a surprisingly rare occurrence – but likely to happen more frequently when restoration of LR2182 is complete!

Cliff Thomas

Works. Hopefully, this will have occurred by the time you read this!

The somewhat bare locomotive will probably have a few test runs on LBR metals before dispatch to the contractor for what will amount to its crowning glory. We have identified a favoured contractor but until a few loose ends are resolved over the drawings of what is required (we want the cupola to be 'right', but a couple of questions over exactly what 'right' actually is, have to be resolved) before a contract is signed. We are now pretty confident restoration of LR2182 will be completed in 2018, possibly by summer.

A stage was reached in 2017 when it looked as though the project would stall for want of finance. Some highly welcome donations and a very reassuring back-up offer avoided this happening, but we are not quite out of the woods. Frankly, every item of expenditure requires a check to see if there is money available to pay the bill and loans may be needed to see things through to a conclusion – with no obvious means of repayment since petrol locos cannot earn their keep with steaming fees!

If you can assist the final stages of returning this unique piece of WW1 light railway history to operation in its as-built form, a donation would be very welcome, please send to The Greensand Railway Museum Trust, c/o Page's Park Station, Billington Road, Leighton Buzzard, Bedfordshire LU7 4TG. If you can also complete a Gift Aid form, we can reclaim the tax and increase the value of your donation by 25%!

GRMT trustees are railway author and journalist Cliff Thomas (chairman), Tony Tomkins, David Smith (all three being founding trustees), Chris Grimes (owner of several locomotives including Avonside Sezela No. 4) and Terry Bendall (ex-officio as current LBR chairman). The late Sir William McAlpine was the Trust's President up to his sad death on March 3.

NANCY
by Darragh Connolly

NANCY in action during her industrial service at the Eastwell Iron Ore Quarries.
Author's Collection

Many of our readers may be familiar with the former Eastwell Iron Ore Quarries Avonside built loco NANCY in 1908. The loco is currently at Alan Keef awaiting completion for a return to steam, to the Cavan and Leitrim Railway at Dromod, Co. Leitrim, Ireland. This update is written by a member of both the railway and the Avonside Nancy Restoration Group.

History

NANCY became works number 1547 of Avonside works and was delivered new to Stanton Ironworks Co. Ltd for use on their Brewer's Grave tramway serving Woolsthorpe Quarries in Lincolnshire. It spent its working life in the ironstone Industry until 1961 when it was bought for preservation by Sterling Bros, a group based

at Watnall, Nottinghamshire. It remained there until 1972 when it was acquired by Lord O'Neill for his Shane's Castle Railway, County Antrim, Northern Ireland with the aim of eventual restoration in partnership with the former British Aluminum Peckett 0-4-0T number TYRONE, and former Bord na Mona Andrew Barclay number 3 (LM45).

NANCY was striped and assesed for restoration at Shane's Castle and languished there for a long period. Lord O'Neill then sold the entirety of the Shane's Castle Railway with much of the stock forming the nucleus of the Giants Causeway and Bushmills Railway. NANCY was bought by the Cavan & Leitrim Railway in 1997, and was brought

Three more views of the pre-preservation era NANCY, the upper view showing it at its first home of Woolsthorpe - note the hole in the chimney!
Midland Railway Trust, Cavan and Leitrim Railway (2)

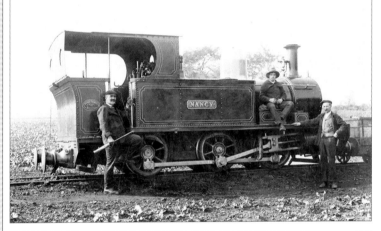

to Dromod in pieces for an assessment on its restoration to take place. The opportunity to send the loco away for restoration came when the remains of NANCY were placed on the low loader that Alan Keef had used to deliver a replica balcony carriage in Cavan and Leitrim style for the Railway. The loco has been at the workshops of Alan Keef Ltd in Ross-on-Wye since 1999, where the restoration has been steadily progressed as funds permitted. To date the Cavan and Leitrim Railway has invested over £145,000 into NANCY, and we are now at the very final stage of restoration.

Dromod

The current preservation scheme at Dromod was established in 1992 under the leadership of the Narrow Gauge Trust. When they first viewed the site as a potential for preservation the only Cavan and Leitrim Railway items remaining were the original station building dating from 1887, the single road engine shed and water tower. The Cavan And Leitrim Railway Co, Ltd was Formed in 1993

The group were successful in obtaining EU grant aid to acquire the former station building and a ¾ mile long section of trackbed along the original alignment as far as Cloncoolry crossing.

Michael Kennedy and Philip Bedford are the primary managers of the railway and undertake its day to day operation, with Michael working full time to provide for the railway. The station site is not home to just locomotives and rolling stock but a cockpit from a Boeing 707, a French army cannon, and several vintage buses including two original Great Northern Railway (Ireland) Gardner buses made at Dundalk, one being fully restored.

Michael had collected several unique railway artefacts including a Tralee and Dingle 3rd class carriage dating from 1891, a Kerr Stuart 0-4-2T DROMAD built in 1916 (originally named SIR MURRAY MORRISON), and several industrial Ruston Hornsby diesel locos that once worked the bogs of Ireland for Bord na Mona.

Services began in 1994 with Kerr Stuart 0-4-2T DROMAD and a former CIE West Clare section railcar trailer, built on a Tralee and Dingle underframe dating from 1890. Steam services ceased in 2004 with DROMAD requiring an overall. The decision was taken to concentrate on completing NANCY, now in 2018 we have the realistic prospect of having NANCY back in steam for the first time in almost 60 years. She will also allow steam services to resume at Dromod, a very welcome development.

NANCY's Restoration

The restoration of NANCY was put on the backburner from 2007 until 2016 because of the recession in Ireland. The recession had a huge effect on Ireland, particularly in the midlands and border counties with a drop in visitor numbers. The Cavan and Leitrim Railway prioritised its day to day operation over NANCY.

NANCY was not forgotten though, and through the dedication of a number of Irish narrow gauge enthusiasts, a support group known as the Avonside Nancy Restoration Group was established circa 2016 to oversee the projects conclusion and return the 3ft-gauge ex-ironstone loco back to a steamable condition. Many of these members are active volunteers with the Cavan and Leitrim and the Stradbally Woodland Railway in County Laois.

Since 1999 the wheelsets have had the tyres re-profiled and returned to the frames, and the cylinders, motion and valve gear are also now complete. Much of the upper structure has required complete renewal, including the boiler, footplates, tanks, cab and bunker.

The group's first major progress was the completion of the new boiler, with the group successfully raising £9,000 (€10,200) within 5 months. The group has continued to progress to the outstanding components required, a new smokebox and ashpan are the last items, then the loco can be re-assembled.

A view of what Nancy looked like after arrival in Dromod circa 1997. It looks a shadow of its former self, the tanks / cab and smokebox were rotten and copies would eventually be made by Alan Keef.
Cavan and Leitrim Railway

It looks likely that NANCY will steam for the first time in 2018 at Alan Keef's Open Day subject to funding and completion. There is approximately €17,000 remaining on returning NANCY to steam - every penny counts.

Lough Swilly Connection

There is a connection between NANCY and one of the former Lough Swilly (LLSR) steam engines, NANCY looks very similar in outline to one of the early LLSR Hawthorn 0-6-0T locos. Michael over the years has collected the whistle and gauge glass from a LLSR engine in his collection, it came from one of the "Big Giants" the Hudswell Clarke 4-8-4T locos. These were the biggest narrow gauge engines to operate in these islands. Once restored people will be able to hear a Lough Swilly engine for the first time since its closure in 1953!

Isle of Man

There is the prospect of NANCY visiting the Isle of Man Steam Railway for the 2019 season, subject to funding and completion. This will give much needed publicity to the Cavan and Leitrim Railway and indeed the Irish Narrow gauge scene.

How to Contribute

We now have the prospect of having NANCY in steam, and in service at Dromod. We can only achieve this with support from members of the public. I would like to thank several members of the Avonside Nancy restoration Group particularly Michael Kennedy, Philip Bedford and all at Dromod, Darragh Connolly, Thomas Fogarty, Glen Murphy Alan Curran and others at the Stradbally Woodland Railway for their hard work and donations, and thanks to all that have contributed.

For those wishing to visit Dromod, we are located in Co. Leitrim and can be accessed by rail from the main Dublin – Sligo railway line, with services operating daily from Dublin Connolly. If you would like to contact Michael for further info please email: dromodrailway@gmail.com

For details on how to donate, visit: https://sites.google.com/site/thecavanandleitrimrailway/-nancy or look at the Facebook page: https://www.facebook.com/groups/irishnarrowgauge/

Acknowledgements

This article was written with assistance from Thomas Fogarty and Michael Kennedy.

THE WESTONZOYLAND LIGHT RAILWAY
by Jason Keswick

Lister Railtruck pulling the Ransome piling winch, the only salvaged narrow gauge rolling stock from the local Rivers Authority used for bank maintenance and repairs and volunteer built box van.

Alan Davies

Westonzoyland Pumping Station was built in 1831, it was the first steam powered pumping station built on the Somerset Levels. Initially with a beam engine and scoop wheel, later replaced in 1861 with an Easton Amos Land Drainage Machine which features an Appold centrifugal pump, capable of lifting 100 tons of water per minute. The pumping station became redundant when it was replaced with a diesel pump alongside. It fell into disrepair until a group from the Somerset Industrial Archaeological Society moved in to tackle the repair work in 1977. From here the Westonzoyland Engine Trust was formed and began to collect what it is now one of the largest collections of stationary steam engines and pumps in the UK.

The idea of building a narrow-gauge railway at the pumping station came about very early on. It was known that the River Board had laid jubilee track along the river banks for maintenance purposes and it was assumed that Wessex Water still had this stored in a local depot. The museums contact then reported that unfortunately it had all been disposed of 12 months before! Since the seed had been sown amongst the volunteers the Trust started looking around (1977) in odd places, either buried in undergrowth or set in concrete!

Various sites were stripped of what we could find including the old Poole Brickworks near Wellington. From here track all set in concrete was dug out using a large road compressor. We also relieved two sets of points, a traverser and three Hudson waggon turntables. Two of these 'turned' out to be 25.5" gauge. It was believed that some track handled skips coming in from the pit, whilst the other, including the traverser had been a hand pushed system taking green tiles and bricks to the drying kilns.

Back at the museum work began on putting some of this track down. Initially it was laid on top of the ground using short lengths of old telephone poles as sleepers. These were sawn down the centre and rails attached with screw bolts. A few V-Skips had been sourced and these were used to help move materials around the site.

One of the first steam engines to be installed was a large horizontal by W F Wills & Co of Bridgwater from a local brickworks. This was being located in the old coal house and it was decided to put a rail line down into this part of the pumping station permanently. A 24" turntable was put in to help get the engine into position. This track work is still as it was laid then and the engine house/coal store provides our only undercover railway storage and is where our three resident locomotives now reside.

It was now considered that the railway was a permanent feature and a visitor attraction in its own right. The Trust was then offered the Simplex 40S from Severn Trent Water Authority where it was used at Minworth Sewage Treatment Plant. This was an ideal acquisition as both Motor Rail Simplex and Listers made locos for the water industry. Rail was continually collected from various sources in various conditions and weights, some of which came from the Dartmoor target railways abandoned by the army.

With the decline in industrial railways, inevitably the next casualty was Fisons Peat Works at Ashcott who were ceasing operation of the narrow gauge railway. Enquiries were made about acquiring a Lister loco. A consortium of members raised the capital needed to purchase one and with help from a friendly local business transport was arranged.

Lister Railtruck and homemade coach with our current Trust President Iain Miles driving and wife our current secretary Mary Miles getting propelled up the line in September 1988.

Iain Miles

The Trust was fortunate in collecting what it did. The scrappies had been in to most sites but luckily rusty light weight rail wasn't worth them considering. The other problem was the number of other dedicated railway groups who were searching the country for rail, so decent stuff was going to them. Sleepers, then as now, were the biggest problem. The luckiest find was courtesy of Wessex Water. A large quantity of 30lb rail was sourced, having never been used for rail track. It was used at Milverton (Somerset) sewage works as a floor to the sand filter. When the filter bed needed changing, the front bucket of JCB was pushed along it thus stopping the bucket from digging in too deeply, some shorter lengths were also found forming a cattle grid at the entrance!

For some time, apart from the occasional movement of a piece of equipment or a steam exhibit the railway fell into disrepair. The wagons were all lined up on a siding with weeds growing up through them. It was with the restoration of a Marshall Portable boiler (2005 - 06) that created a revival in the railway. The small amount of timber needed to fire the original Coltman vertical boiler on site was stored outside the boiler house. However the Marshall would consume much more and the site insurance company ruled that combustible materials shouldn't be stored alongside the listed building. A wood pile was established at the extreme limit of our site (which is long and narrow). It was soon realised that the railway should be brought back into use to transport cut timber from the pile right to the back of the boiler. The existing railway had additional sleepers added to improve it and it had some new gravel added for support. The work was carried out with materials available on site. A wagon turntable was removed from outside the exhibition hall doors to allow an extension to this spur right up to the Marshall. Initially a wagon was converted with a timber frame to support the load, however it was later decided to convert a whole fleet and steel uprights were added along with steel plate decks. Pallets and cut waste wood could then be stacked up and unloaded directly into the boiler. On a good steaming over 75 pallets were being consumed which was at least 3-4 loaded wagons. Each one being delivered and the empties taken away creating a true working industrial railway!

The Lister Railtruck taking another wagon of cut timber towards the boiler siding Lister Railtruck taking another wagon of cut timber towards the boiler siding.

Alan Davies

We were then approached by the Somerset and Dorset Railway Trust based on the West Somerset Railway at Washford. They also have a Lister from Fisons peat works and a few wagons. They had a stack of heavy gauge mining track panels that they no longer wanted. These were collected and soon formed an extension further down the site to our relocated timber pile allowing us to increase our visitor parking. It was very noticeable how much better the heavier weight rail looked and felt to travel on than the mostly 14lb rail on the rest of the railway.

The Trust had once provided passenger trips on a small man rider, but this was disposed of when the railway fell out of use. Thoughts turned to the possibility of offering rides to visitors again and with some experiments on a new open wagon built by one the volunteers it was clear that it would be a hit! The permanent way was clearly going to need improvements and sleepers were beginning to become very rotten. A visit by volunteers to the Hampton & Kempton Waterworks Railway at its early stage gave us the idea to make sleepers in concrete. Some tests went ahead and a suitable mould was made. Three versions were installed and proved very satisfactory. However the process was slow and the sleepers very heavy. Our attention turned to the big pile of 30lb rail mentioned earlier from a Wessex Water site. It was clear that this rail would give us a much better permanent way. Our hand was eventually forced when work on an extension to our café required the installation of a new underground mains supply... the only suitable route being underneath the railway for a large section of it. After some chatting with various people, a conversation with Alan Keef Ltd opened up the possibility to purchase a large supply of steel sleepers from the Woodhead Tunnels system. Keef's had been carrying out a maintenance contract and these sleepers had been removed. Not all were usable but at least 90% were still very serviceable, the plus side being they were for 30lb rail! Sleepers purchased, rails on site we began stripping the old railway, ducting was installed and a new ballast bed of clean 40mm limestone was laid and the huge task of laying the railway from scratch began! Most of our volunteers had never worked on track as our existing hadn't been touched properly in years. It was a big learning curve but we soon got the hang of it. To make the railway more usable a loop was formed using an existing 25lb point and a donated 25lb point from the Leadhills and Wanlockhead Railway kindly collected by our Chairman one weekend!

Pandrol Clips & Steel Sleepers made fast work of replacing the corner through to the car park level crossing.

Both: Alan Davies

Volunteers get to grips with laying the 30lb rail and pressed steel sleepers. A larger Jim Crow was borrowed to assist in bending the rail.

Alan Davies

Once the first section was completed, we purchased some more sleepers from Keef's, this time new with pandrol clips which took us from our new loop around the corner through our 'cutting' to our pedestrian level crossing. This being completed just in time for one of our railway galas where one of the 'Taxi' Andrew Barclay locomotives from the WHHR at Porthmadog was visiting. At present this is as far as we have got with track work. We have one curve left to replace and then the whole running line will be built from 30lb rail and steel sleepers.

Plans are underway to extend the line at the far end of the site behind a set of flood gates to a platform. This will mean the railway covers the full extent of the site. We are just securing an additional 75m of 30lb rail and more metal sleepers to achieve this. A few sets of 25lb points have also recently been collected from Launceston Steam Railway that will allow a siding to be taken off the loop. This siding will be destined to enter a Nissen Hut that is to be donated allowing further covered storage and space for visiting locomotives including (hopefully) a steam engine in the future!

All this work has paid off, the Trust was able to acquire a bogie coach chassis from the Cleethorpes Coast Light Railway. As you can tell a pattern is emerging here, there is very little narrow gauge equipment in the South West and so we have to travel some distance to get what we need! The chassis was returned to the museum where volunteers set about restoring it. The main chassis was quite narrow and it was felt that it could be widened. A cut and shut job was performed and everything cleaned up and painted. Treated decking was used to form the floor and seats as we knew it would have to live outside. It was then decided to create

Ex Creekmoor Light Railway Coach after rebuilding at Westonzoyland in 2015.

Author

the body panels from aluminium composite wrapped in vehicle vinyl. Having painted other wagons, the longevity of the vinyl in the sun is impressive and being low cost any damage can be repaired by removing the panel, stripping the vinyl and re-wrapping. Sign writing was added in vinyl again, this all being produced by a volunteer. The coach was launched and became an instant hit. During restoration, we were contacted by an ex. volunteer of the Creekmoor Light Railway, no longer in existence that was based in Dorset between 1968 – 78. The coach was built by him with bogies from brick carrying chassis. It is understood that it was involved in a run-away train on an incline, luckily being on the Somerset Levels this isn't an issue!

Although the Westonzoyland Pumping Station Museum is not dedicated to narrow gauge railways, the railway at the museum is an integral part of the story of land drainage and the industries of Somerset with industrial systems often being used in land drainage schemes, bank maintenance and industrial

sites where many of our steam engines once worked. Now we can offer passenger rides it has become an attraction in its own right. We have started a Narrow Gauge Gala held on August Bank Holiday where we run a selection of passenger and industrial freight trains. The Trust is going to continue to invest in improvements and extending the line. Most recently one of our volunteers has restored a Lister Railtruck that once operated at John Board & Co Cement and Limeworks at Bridgwater, Somerset and is on loan to the museum which will also be followed by an F.C Hibbered Planet Y-Type locomotive currently being restored off-site. This loco is not local but an identical type that is now at the Steeple Grange Light Railway was used in a local Somerset brickworks. Apart from the small collection of items at the Somerset & Dorset Railway Trusts site, Westonzoyland is thought to be the only site open to the public in Somerset displaying and operating local narrow gauge equipment and for that matter in the South West of England.

The resident Simplex 40S pulling the new passenger wagon and box van.

Visiting Barclay 'Taxi' from the WHHR for one of the railway's gala events on August Bank Holiday Monday with two visiting original peat wagons from Fisons, Somerset on loan from the Somerset & Dorset Railway Trust

A misty Somerset Levels showing the new 30lb layout with the Simplex & Lister on the loop with an open wagon with garden clippings, box van and passenger coach..
All: Alan Davies

NARROW GAUGE 2017

Three views of narrow gauge steam in 2017 - (Left) Quarry Hunslet STATFOLD waits impatiently at its home base; (Above) Visiting Bure Valley Railway No. 1 WROXHAM BROAD pilots resident DOCTOR SYN during the RHDR's May Gala Weekend; (Below) 823 COUNTESS heads an authentic replica GWR-era train through Sylfaen halt during the Welshpool & Llanfair's Annual Gala.

Peter Donovan, Keith Frewin, Alan Frewin

THE TRAINS FROM SPAIN
by Mike Bent

Between 1925 and 1950 Locomotivfabriken Krauß & Comp. of München (later Krauss-Maffei) built 18 381 mm (15 inch) gauge 4-6-2 steam locomotives, mostly for temporary railways laid in parks and international exhibition sites. Of these 1/3 scale machines, seven were sent to Spain in the late 1920s... and now only two remain there.

Spain's Narrower Gauges

We tend to associate railways in Spain with 'broad' - 1,668 mm (formerly 1,674 mm) gauge – tracks. Naturally, there is now a growing network of 1,435 mm gauge lines, most of these built over the past three decades or so for high speed services. Spain also has extensive metre gauge networks, while the number of lines of narrower gauges (such as 750, 650 and 600 mm) built to serve mining and industrial complexes

One of the original Barcelona locomotives, NÚRIA in the guise of LISA, on the Dresdner Parkeisenbahn on 11 September 2010.

Henry Mühlpfordt
via Wikimedia Commons

was legion. The 1,668/1,435mm dual gauge three-rail network is on the increase, while over a century ago in Asturias there were stretches of 650/1,674mm dual gauge, and even some industrial networks with three gauges! The narrowest gauge believed to have been used for industrial lines was 460 mm, examples existing at Cabárceno (south of Santander) and at Dicido, near Castro-Urdiales.

Over the past couple of decades even narrower gauges have proliferated, thanks to the activities of various enthusiast societies, who have endeavoured to bring something f the atmosphere of 'real' railway travel and un to a modern society fed on a continual, and rather sterile diet of car travel, combined erhaps with the occasional dose of AVEs, EMUs and DMUs. Most of these railways re in Catalunya, emphasising the fact that Catalunya is in many ways 'different' to the 'est' of Spain. A few other examples can be found elsewhere. Gauges vary between 254 mm, 184mm and 127 mm, and operating days are irregular and unpredictable – mainly weekends and public holidays, since these lines are run by volunteers. Perhaps one day we can take a closer look at some of them in a future article. But for the moment et us focus on the chequered careers of those Krauss-built Pacifics which went to Spain, and which even now are making ailway history...

Barcelona Exposición Internacional 1929

In 1905 the architect Josep Puig i Cadafalch proposed an international exhibition in the Catalan capital. A definitive project, making use of Montjuic, the steep-sided hill overlooking the port area, was presented in 1915 and development on the ground began the same year. To facilitate construction a 3 km 600 mm gauge railway was laid, initially with Decauville rail, later with 10 kg/m Vignole rail. With an altitude difference of 62 m along the route, gradients as steep as 5% were required, and the line was electrified at 220 V DC, using a three-phase system (the Barcelona grid supply was 6,000 V DC). The catenary had two conductor wires, and the third conductor took the form of a third rail. Two three-tonne, two-axle locomotives, each powered by two 15 HP traction motors giving a total tractive effort of 500 kg, were supplied by H. Peter. They were baptised Catalunya and Barcelona and hauled rakes of platform wagons supplied by Orenstein & Koppel. Animal traction was used on the various temporary branches laid to access different parts of the site. Once the exposition complex was nearing completion, in the late 1920s, the contractors' railway

was dismantled and the locomotives were scrapped.

Meanwhile, a second railway was being built, for public use during the Expo. 2.1 km in length, it ran through the central part of the exhibition area, encircling four abandoned quarries. The principal civil engineering features were a 12 m long tunnel and a 20 m bridge, just to the north of the main station, which was adjacent to the amusement park and Tyrolean restaurant, in the largest of the quarries. There were also two halts, one serving the Palacio Nacional, the other the Palacio de Misiones. Maximum gradient was a fierce 6% between these two halts. A round trip cost 1.50 pesetas, a run between a pair of stations, 50 céntimos.

The motive power was sourced from Germany. Following a study tour in England (home of Sir Arthur Heywood's 381 mm 'Minimum Gauge' railway) in the early 1920s, the engineer Roland Martens designed a 1:3.33 scale, 381 mm gauge 4-6-2 Pacific, and in 1925 Krauss built three locomotives of this type, which were first exhibited at the transport trade fair in München, then in 1926 at the GESOLEI (Grosse Ausstellung für Gesundheitspflege, Soziale Fürsorge und Liebesübungen) exhibition in Düsseldorf and in 1928 at the PRESSA exhibition in Köln. In 1928 they were bought by Enrich Brangsch, of Leipzig, who ran a company specialising in the construction of Feldbahnen and similar railways for use at exhibitions throughout Germany and central Europe. Brangsch was engaged by the Barcelona Expo organisers to realise the tracklaying and signalling of the railway, and he also supplied the locomotives, on hire. These were temporarily named NÚRIA, MONTSERRAT and BARCELONA. The passenger carriages, which rode on Jakobs articulated bogies, were supplied by Wumag of Görlitz (now Bombardier). A very brief Pathétone video available on YouTube (https://www.youtube.com/watch?v=Lv7Xbv4MeaU) shows a lively MONTSERRAT performing.

The Expo ran from 20 May 1929 to 15 January 1930, and ran up a loss of 180 million pesetas, this in part attributable to

Outside the International Expo Palace, on Montjuic, Barcelona 1929.
Josep Branguli collection

the fact that the Wall Street Crash happened on 29 October 1929, and the number of participants and visitors fell sharply after that. After the gates had closed for the final time, the three locomotives were returned to Germany, being used at various events throughout Europe until the outbreak of the Second World War. Among the locations they probably travelled to, either individually or collectively, were Antwerpen (1930), Dresden (1930, 1931, 1936, 1937), Cork (1931), Berlin (1931), Essen (1938) and Stuttgart (1939). During the war they were stored in a shed in Kamenz (between Dresden and Bautzen), being subjected to full overhauls between 1945 and 1950 by VEB Baumechanik of Leipzig-Engelsdorf. All three were present at the garden festival in Erfurt in July and August 1950, then (see table) were moved to the park railways in Leipzig and Dresden, where they remain to this day. The rolling stock and infrastructure from the Barcelona line were dismantled and used by Brangsch at other exhibitions in various parts of Europe.

This was not quite the end of the railway story on Montjuic. In the early 1960s a Venezuelan, José Antonio Borges Villegas, obtained a 30-year concession from the city council to build an amusement park, which covering an area of around 100,000 m², was inaugurated in 1965. One of its attractions was the Tren del Oeste, a 400 m long 600 mm gauge line in dumb-bell shape, an oddity being that the central section, between the two 'bells', had three rails, the centre one shared by the wheels of trains traversing it in each direction. The station was situated on a curve on one of the 'bells'. Originally Villegas envisaged acquiring a steam locomotive (at that time he would have had plenty of choice, given the number of industrial systems still active in Spain), but in the end he opted for a 'steam outline' diesel, built in 1964 by A. Herschell & Co. of Buffalo in the USA. Bearing the works number 5241364, externally it was identical to the classic Western 4-4-0, although in reality it had a B-2-B arrangement, with a four-cylinder diesel and mechanical transmission. The driving wheels had a diameter of 300 mm, the non-powered ones, 610 mm. It bore the name IRON HORSE, and on its tender vere the words Tren del Oeste. Five open bogie carriages were acquired, each with a capacity of eight passengers (40 per train). The fare in 1990 was 200 pesetas, and the round trip took four minutes, certainly one of the more expensive train journeys, given the distance per peseta, in Spain at that time! The park closed in 1998, all the rides were dismantled, and the gardens which have since been developed on the site are named after the poet Joan Brossa.

Exposición Iberoamericana de Sevilla (1929)

This event ran from 9 May 1929 to 21 June 1930, and to convey visitors from one part of the vast complex to another a 381 mm gauge railway was built. It was said that the railway was the gift of Alfonso XIII to the city, though it appears that three of the four locomotives were probably acquired through the efforts of José Cruz Conde Fustegueras, the former Mayor of Córdoba, the Civil Governor of Sevilla province between 1926 and 1931, and the organiser of the EXPO, following his visit to the PRESSA exhibition in Köln in 1928.

The railway offered a circular run of about 5 km from the Casino de la Exposición to the southern part of the grounds. There were five stations – Glorieta Bécquer, Paseo de las Delicias, Galerías Comerciales, Barrio Moro, Parque de Atracciones and Plaza de América. An extension loop was later built along the Avenida de Venezuela to the sports stadium and circling the huge livestock exhibition area, though it was used only when activities were taking place in this part of the grounds. Four steam locomotives, SEVILLA, SANTA MARÍA, PINTA and NIÑA (see table 1), were supplied by Krauss, capable of hauling rakes of ten carriages accommodating up to 160 passengers, and reaching a top speed of 30 km/h. In all 40 carriages were acquired, these also being articulated vehicles, mounted on Jakobs bogies.

In 1929 523,217 passengers were carried, the standard fare being one peseta, and the trains covered 36,062 km. During the entire 14-month exposition they clocked up receipts of 684,000 pesetas, only superseded by those generated by the hire of sites for commercial activities (787,000 pesetas) and the sale of entrance tickets (1.6 million pesetas). But the exposition as a whole ran up debts of around 40 million pesetas!

After the event had closed, the locomotives and rolling stock were stored in the depot, situated at the junction where the Avenida de la Borbolla enters the Plaza de España. They were used on at least two more occasions, during the Feria de San Miguel in September 1930 and on 14 April 1932, to celebrate the founding of the Republic. On 23 September 1933 the Exposition's winding-up committee put the stock up for sale for 114,400 pesetas, but it is not known whether any interest was shown in it. Some of the city councillors made an attempt to revive the line, and in 1935, following discussions with the owners of an amusement park in Madrid, it was proposed to create something similar in the vicinity of the Plaza de España. The proposals, involving purchase of the stock for 90,000 pesetas, and a 20-year municipal concession, were sanctioned by the winding-up committee on 30 January 1936. However, the victory of the Popular Front in the elections the following month resulted in the scheme being abandoned, and the construction of the Nationalist military headquarters in the Plaza de España the following year meant the demolition of the depot. Almost all the stock was dismantled and eventually housed in the very humid municipal stores under the Puerta Carmona, while the track was sold for scrap for 20,000 pesetas. Over the following decades rust took its toll. Curiously, NIÑA and two carriages were discovered in late 1963 in an obscure outdoor location near the Plaza de España, and the following year were provisionally plinthed in the Blanca Nieves (Snow White) children's park, which was situated near the present-day Santa Justa station. The rest of the stock was auctioned by the municipality in 1966, fetching 30 céntimos per kilo (55,000 pesetas in total) as scrap, and was transferred to a scrapyard in the Urbanización Arroyo de la Plata.

Life after the Expo...

In the early 1980s the Asociación Sevillana de Amigos del Ferrocarril proposed salvaging some of the material for use on a 2 km circuit in the Parque de María Luisa, and requested municipal support. The Mayor, Luis Uruñuela, was interested in the scheme, but very little came of it. NIÑA and one of the surviving carriages were cosmetically restored in 1983 in readiness for the 'Sevilla y su Tren' exhibition, which took place between 7 and 17 April that year, and were exhibited on a short stretch of curved track on the patio outside one of the city's palaces. NIÑA was then plinthed in Plaza de Armas terminus. The latter was closed on 30 September 1990 as part of the remodelling of the urban rail network in Sevilla in connection with the arrival of the

high speed line from Madrid. In Novembe that year, when the tracks in the terminus were lifted, NIÑA was moved by lorry to RENFE's San Pablo EMU/DMU depot and works, (see the YouTube video https://www.youtube.com/watch?v=3pjdOZyDYZA). She was then exhibited in 1998 at the Palacic de Congresos y Exposiciones as part o the 'Territorio Ferroviario' exhibition to commemorate 150 years of public railways in Spain, and then in 2000 moved to the new Sevilla Santa Justa station (dating from 1992) where she was re-plinthed, on the platform between tracks 8 and 9, adjacent to the clubrooms belonging to the Asociación Sevillana de Amigos del Ferrocarril. She could conceivably be restored to working order, since she lacks no components Plaza de Armas terminus, duly restored now houses a collection of shops and restaurants.

Salvation (or was it purgatory?) came in June 1969 for SANTA MARÍA, PINTA and SEVILLA when the management of the new

Possibly still operational at the time, SANTA MARÍA at the Casa de Campo circuit in Madrid in 1978.

Author's collection

Casa de Campo amusement park and trade air complex in Madrid announced that it had bought them. SANTA MARÍA was returned to service on the 381 mm gauge circular line there on 14 May 1970. SEVILLA was rebuilt as a diesel locomotive, donating some surplus components to the other two machines, to keep them operational. In the late 1970s or early 1980s SANTA MARÍA was hired by El Corte Inglés department store chain in Barcelona, restored to working order and used for a while together with a carriage to offer rides on a very short stretch of track outside the shop, El Corte Inglés also taking the locomotive, carriage and track to Murcia and Málaga as an attraction outside the latter's department stores. It is possible that the locomotive also visited other cities as part of the promotional campaign.

In 1995/6 Martín Atracciones, which is a manufacturer of rides and equipment

The Americanised and dieselised SEVILLA, with PINTA's tender, in action at the Casa de Campo circuit in Madrid.
Josep Branguli collection

for theme and amusement parks, rebuilt SEVILLA in the style of a Wild West locomotive. According to the company's website report, by that time all that remained serviceable were the underframe, wheels, and coupling rods. A new boiler (housing the diesel), new brakes, cab and tender were built, but the tender carried the name PINTA!

However, around the turn of the millennium it was decided to install a new fairground attraction within the area enclosed by the railway circuit. For safety reasons, a level crossing with barriers was necessary, to give the general public access to this, so it was decided to close the railway, PINTA being stored, temporarily, in the line's artificial tunnel. Once again the fate of the three locomotives hung in the balance, all three having been moved to the park's storage and maintenance equipment yard in Brunete, in the outer suburbs of western Madrid.

To Catalunya... and Beyond

Salvation came in 2002 in the form of the Ferrocarril del Maresme, of Mataró, near Barcelona. This group of engineers and railway enthusiasts had plans to build a 381 mm gauge railway somewhere on the Maresme coast, to the northeast of Barcelona, but failed to gain local authority support. In May 2002 all three locomotives, together with some of the carriages were moved to the company's workshop in Mataró.

From this point on it is practically impossible to refer to the locomotives by name, since tenders were exchanged. The best guide to identities are the works numbers. At the time of the move to Mataró their status was as follows:

- 8455 (originally PINTA, but now with SANTA MARÍA's tender): Having been a plinthed exhibit prior to closure of the line, she was still in reasonable external condition.

- 8457 (originally SANTA MARÍA) was little more than a rusting kit of parts,

Table 1: Krauss, Krauss-Maffei and Krupp 381 mm Gauge Locomotives

Builder	Works No.	Year	Current Location	Name/Number, notes
Krauss	8351	1925	Dresdner Parkeisenbahn	001 LISA ex-NÚRIA
Krauss	8352	1925	Leipziger Parkeisenbahn	03 215 (later 03 002) ex-MONTSERRAT
Krauss	8353	1925	Dresdner Parkeisenbahn	003 MORITZ ex-BARCELONA
Krauss	8441	1928	Prater Liliputbahn (Wien)	Da1 BRIGITTE
Krauss	8442	1928	Prater Liliputbahn (Wien)	Da2 GRETE
Krauss	8443	1928	Various exhibition sites until 1940, fate unknown	Sold to Brangsch
Krauss	8444	1928	Various exhibition sites until 1940, fate unknown	Sold to Brangsch
Krauss	8445	1928	Prater Liliputbahn (Wien)	Rebuilt as diesel 1960/1
Krauss	8455	1929	Killesbergbahn, Stuttgart	SANTA MARÍA ex-PINTA
Krauss	8456	1929	Sevilla Santa Justa	NIÑA
Krauss	8457	1929	Ravenglass & Eskdale Railway	SANTA MARÍA, now WHILLAN BECK
Krauss	8473	1929	Mataró	SEVILLA
Krupp	1662	1937	Waveney Valley Railway (Bressingham)	ROSENKAVALIER
Krupp	1663	1937	Waveney Valley Railway (Bressingham)	MÄNNERTREU
Krupp	1937	1937	Romney, Hythe and Dymchurch Railway	11 BLACK PRINCE, ex-FLEISSIGES LIESCHEN
Krauss-Maffei	17655	1950	National Bal Bhavan Park (New Delhi)	Not in service
Krauss-Maffei	17674	1950	Killesbergbahn (Stuttgart)	SPRINGERLE
Krauss-Maffei	17675	1950	Killesbergbahn (Stuttgart)	TAZZELWURM

Consigned to semi-darkness, but at least safe from hooligans and graffiti-sprayers. NIÑA (8456) at Sevilla-Santa Justa station in May 2016.

Gerry Balding

since she had been moved to Brunete in the early 1990s.

- 8473 (SEVILLA, with PINTA's tender), was reasonably intact, but was no longer a steam locomotive, having lost her original smokebox, boiler and cab.
- At least four carriages were rescued. These had been grounded, but their Jakobs bogies also survived, rusting.

The salvage team then managed to obtain all documentation that existed on the Krauss 381 mm gauge Pacifics. Helge Hufschläger, the Archives Director at Krauss-Maffei, supplied all the surviving blueprints, while much advice on braking systems and safety aspects of operation was provided by Thomas Jacob, the technical director of the Dresdner Parkeisenbahn.

First to be fully restored to working order (and tested in steam on the workshop's own test bench) was 8455, which made its public debut at the AutoRetro veteran vehicle exhibition in Barcelona in 2005. In autumn 2014 she was sold to the Killesbergbahn in Stuttgart, and since 2016 has been in service there, having had the bottom of her boiler replaced following rusting on account of water having been left there in between infrequent steamings while in Madrid. She now carries the name SANTA MARÍA above her underframe – and not on her tender – although she was of course originally PINTA. She can be seen being delivered and in action in the Eisenbahn-Romantik documentary: https://www.youtube.com/watch?v=DaWt74I2SbY.

Our story now moves to the Lake District,

to the Ravenglass & Eskdale Railway, which in the early 1990s sent two of its workers, Geoff Holland and Chris Mounsey, to the undergrowth in the yard at Brunete to see what could be recovered from 8457. The railway company was then looking for another locomotive, and finally decided on SIAN, from the Fairbourne Railway, in 1994. SIAN was eventually overhauled at Ravenglass, but has been fairly nomadic since then, currently being based at Windmill Farm, near Ormskirk.

Meanwhile, in Mataró, the Ferrocarril del Maresme staff embarked upon the huge project of restoring 8457 to working order. Their activities attracted the attention of the R&ER in mid-2015, with a review team visiting the workshops on 19 October that year to assess the condition of the locomotive. Certain design modifications were specified, and the Ferrocarril del Maresme offered to sell for 200,000 EUR, mentioning that interest in 8457 had also been expressed by other groups from Russia and China. At that time the locomotive had not been tested in motion. It was reckoned that transport from Mataró to Ravenglass would cost around 2,500 EUR for the journey of around 2,000 km. The kit of parts which was once SEVILLA was also offered for sale for 100,000 EUR, and still awaits a buyer.

Following a fundraising campaign, the R&ER's 'Train from Spain' left Mataró early in 2016, and upon arrival at the Old Hall Engineering works in Bouth, Cumbria, in February, work started at once to complete restoration, this estimated to cost £126,000.

The main design modification is the provision of a seat in the tender for the driver, to provide protection from flying sparks and cinders. R&ER members voted on a new name, WHILLAN BECK being chosen, after a watercourse crossed by the railway near Dalegarth. Over 50% of members also voted that the 'Midland red' livery carried by 8457 should be changed to Caledonian Railway blue. Repainting was in progress in early September 2017.

Table 2: Principal Technical Data Krauss Locomotives

Number built	15
Years	1925 - 1950
Wheel arrangement	4-6-2
Gauge	381 mm
Length (locomotive)	7430 mm
Width	1000 mm
Height (including chimney)	1400 mm
Height (to boiler centre)	900 mm
Height (to buffer centres)	315 mm
Driving wheel diameter	530 mm
All other wheels, diameter	300 mm
Rigid wheelbase	1250 mm
Minimum curve radius negotiable	20 m
Boiler diameter	600 mm
Tubes - number	56
Tubes - diameter	32 mm
Tubes - length	2200 mm
Heating surface area	11 m^2
Grate surface area	0.44 m^2
Cylinder diameter	150 mm
Cylinder stroke	200 mm
Locomotive weight	5.6 tonnes
Tender weight	2.5 tonnes
Water capacity (tender)	750 litres
Coal capacity (tender)	250 kg

Power rating	22 kW
Maximum service speed	30 km/h

The Krupp-built machines have slightly different technical specifications.

The careers of all the Krauss, Krauss-Maffei and Krupp 381 mm gauge Pacifics are described in detail in:

Eisenbahn-Romantik   Killesbergbahn:
h t t p s : / / w w w . y o u t u b e . c o m /
watch?v=TYP6HUEDRB0
http://www.parkeisenbahn-dresden.de/
index.php?snav52&liliputlokomotiven

The active members of the Krauss / Krupp fleet can be found at the following location:

Dresdner Parkeisenbahn: completed 1950, 5.6 km long, five stations. https://www.parkeisenbahn-dresden.de
Leipziger Parkeisenbahn: completed 1951, 1.9 km, circling the Auensee, a former gravel pit dating from 1909 when Leipzig Hbf. was built. http://www.parkeisenbahn-auensee-leipzig.de
Prater Liliputbahn: completed 1928, extended 1933, 4 km, four stations. http://www.liliputbahn.com
Killesbergbahn: completed 1939, 2.3 km, http://killesbergbahn.de
Ravenglass & Eskdale Railway: completed 1875, converted to 381 mm gauge 1915, 11.3 km, nine stations. https://ravenglass-railway.co.uk
Waveney Valley Railway: completed 1973, 2.5 km circuit within Bressingham gardens http://www.bressingham.co.uk/explore/family-fun.aspx?id=28
Romney, Hythe and Dymchurch Railway: completed 1927, 21.7 km, eight stations. http://www.rhdr.org.uk
National Bal Bhavan Park (New Delhi): Completed in the late 1950s, about 1.6 km circuit. The Krauss is apparently out of service. This unusual transport-related educational centre can be visited at: http://nationalbalbhavan.nic.in/attractions/toy-train.html

A steam test of 8457 (soon to become WHILLAN BECK) was realised at Ravenglass in November 2016.
Keith Herbert

The image which decided WHILLAN BECK's future Caledonian Railway blue livery. There were six livery choices – R&ERPS members were mainly in favour of this.
Ben Vincer

CROSSNESS PUMPING STATION RAILWAYS
by Robin Parkinson

The Outfall Works Enlargement of 1912-1914. Bagnall locomotive GLADYS (No. 1740 of 1903) can be seen.
Mark Smithers collection

Response in parliament to the complaint of the "Great Stink" of 1858, was the catalyst for the design of London's major sewer system. The Crossness Pumping Station was built as part of the Victorian capital's urgently needed drainage sewage system, the sanitation engineering concept designed in 1860's by the visionary Sir. Joseph Bazalgette, opened 1865. The site represents a special example of Victorian engineering and today is one of only two remaining Grade I listed industrial buildings in south east London, which became the forerunner of major sewage works to be later adopted throughout England.

The Crossness Engines Trust was established in 1987 to safeguard the future of the buildings and through the support of grant giving bodies, such as Historic England and The Heritage Lottery Fund and a committed group of volunteers the site has been restored, one engine PRINCE CONSORT steamed again in 2003 to provide a working museum, visitor centre and exhibition space to tell the story of the London's sewer system and its development, including the creation of an outdoor working museum that celebrates industrial heritage. The narrow gauge railway under construction will complement the access walkway, named "John Ridley Way", in the long term it is hoped that the railway will become an attraction in its own right.

1893 map of the 3ft gauge system.
Crossness Engines Trust archive

Since its inception in 1860 by Sir Joseph Bazalgette, Crossness Pumping Station has been supported by rail transport for construction materials handling, steam boiler coal from the wharf, and ash removal to waiting barges. It is hoped that within the next two years another, a new dual gauge line of 18/24" will be completed, this time the first to transport passengers, seen by some as "the cathedral express". Planning permission has now been granted by The London Borough of Bexley in conjunction with the approval of site owners Thames Water Plc. to lay a 700 meter track which almost follows the alignment of the former temporary construction railways built to aid the construction of the sewage works during the late nineteenth century, running from the mainline tracks at Plumstead station.

The Southern High Level Sewer construction of 1904/06 used this original alignment to bring in the materials for the construction of this majestic sewer from Plumstead station. It is believed that this standard gauge line has been laid and lifted at least three times. The construction of the first railway by Lucas & Aird in the 1860's has been confirmed by current research however it is proven that this Plumstead – Crossness contractors line did not join into the metals of the Greenwich & Gravesend Railway Company, stopping some 200 yards north of their tracks, with a loading platform, head shunt, engine shed and water cistern, shown on the Ordnance Survey map (25" scale) of 1867/69 in the National Library of Scotland archives.

When the "Additional Pumping Power Contract" of 1912/14 was awarded to contractor Dick Kerr & Co. during this works at least three short standard gauge lines were laid around the works for steam the cranes used in excavation. In addition the following conventional construction methods of those days a narrow gauge railway was installed to carry away the spoil. Motive power for this was by WG Bagnall (0-4-0ST) 2 foot gauge No. 1740 of 1903, GLADYS, which had previously been with Wrexham & East Denbighshire Water Works, and was first acquired by Dick Kerr in 1912, find her in the 1912/14 Works Enlargement picture.

One of the early London County Council maps that titled CROSSNESS OUTFALL

WG Bagnall loco GLADYS at Crossness in 1912 with a load of cast iron conduits.
Allan C Baker collection

The Hibberd Pony Loco in 1955 – note the tipping skip bogie left.
Crossness Engines Trust archive

WORKS date 1893, shows the whole site with its own, busy tramways of 3ft. 0in. gauge delivering coal from the barges [5000 tons/year] and removing ash to waiting lighters at the river's edge, some of these tramways were shown as running inside a larger tramway of 4' 8", thought installed for the Hydraulic crane. It is believed that the motive power for the tramway was by horse and this is backed up by stables shown on a map of the eastern flank, although from the complexity of the points and curves would have been tricky to navigate with an "Equine Tractor". No photographs remain to show the horse or whether the rails were conventional [raised] or level with the road. Sometime in the 1930's, date uncertain, mechanical tractive power arrived in the form of a Pony Loco by makers F. C. Hibberd of Park Royal, London. This un-numbered & unnamed loco originally built for Duckham's Oil, Portsmouth was (4ft 0in. gauge) , powered by an 8hp JAP petrol engine and thought to have two speeds, forward & reverse, believed scrapped around 1958, a photo taken in 1955 shows her on rails, alongside the frames of a tipping skip wagon. It is unclear as to when the 3ft. gauge system tracks were lifted.

Next door in the Royal Arsenal Woolwich (now Thamesmead Housing Development) was the hugely complex system of the Royal Arsenal Railway with some 140 miles of single and dual gauge track, covering over 1300 acres. In 1915 the Ministry of Munitions placed an order with the Avonside Engine Company, Bristol for sixteen narrow gauge locomotives of the Charlton Class configured as (O-4-OT). These were to be the last class of narrow gauge steam locomotives purchased for use on the Royal Arsenal Railway (RAR). The first six, BRISTOL, GLASGOW, LIVERPOOL, NEWCASTLE, DERBY and WOOLWICH were oil-fired and allocated to work in what were classified as "Danger Buildings" such as the Magazines and Filling Factories. The remaining ten were coal fired, allocated to duties in Non-Danger areas such as coal and passenger haulage. All of this class were fitted with conical spark arrestors but there were other subtle physical differences. All the Class were constructed with outside frames to accommodate the 25in. diameter wheels, set at the Arsenal narrow gauge of 18in. and the now standard axle's centres of 3ft. 3in. Operating at a steam pressure of 160 lbs/sq. in. Walschaerts valve gear was employed to the 8½ dia. by 12in. stroke cylinders. The oil-fired units had a side tank water capacity of 260 gallons, boiler feed by two Craven & Chesham injectors. The rear portion of each tank sectioned off for 50 gallons of light fuel oil, which was preheated via a steam coil before atomisation through a Kermode burner. At one point during the shortages of war the Ministry of Munitions obtained some 400,000 tons of creosote oil to be used as mixed fuel for the oil burners, this was not found entirely suitable, causing problems with naphthalene crystals forming in the pipework, and heavy soot contamination of the boiler tubes. Overall the Charlton's were a sturdy and presentable locomotive, they were quite happy to work around curves of 35ft. radius and could even manage a tight bend of 25ft. if required.

In the mid-1920s after the First World War manufacturing had declined at the Royal Arsenal, many locos of both gauges were sold or cut up for scrap. The Charlton disposals, all were still there in 1931, thirteen had gone by 1934, by 1936 only, NEWCASTLE, WOOLWICH MANCHESTER remained, the latter was scrapped in 1954, the final survivor WOOLWICH was put into storage on sidings in 1954 before being disposed of in 1960 to dealers Messrs E.L. Pitt & Co. of Brackley, Northampton, having been extensively overhauled and possibly a new boiler fitted during her last days at the Arsenal. Photographs exist showing the boiler complete with smokebox and conical chimney after major repair work, standing in building D.59 Blacksmiths Shop, date 1956. This was confirmed by a visitor to Crossness six years ago, this gentleman had just completed his apprenticeship in 56 and one of his first tasks was to roll the angle rings seen wrapping the boiler at either end, to support the lagging skin.

During her time at the Northampton yard, the conical spark arrestor chimney was replaced with one of conventional design. In April 1962 she was put back into steam, on blocks by Engineers J & W. Gower of Bedford, prior to proving and sale, then moved to Devon on 11th April 1962. There she was to assist with track laying and run on the newly constructed 18" gauge line at The Bicton Woodlands Railway. In Devon an air braking system was fitted to be compliant with the HMRI regulations at the time, this compressed air was generated by a Stuart steam pump, mounted on the rear of the cab. To accommodate the air reservoir, the rear cab wall & floor was extended back some 6" from original location and the receiver tank welded to the cab floor. The believed authentic original RAR livery of green lined out with yellow was changed to blue with yellow lining, the original colour was never found as the 16 coats of paint teased off by the CET restoration team.

Unlike so many of our heritage locomotives that have rusted to oblivion, or have been cut up for scrap, WOOLWICH was well cared for in the last 40 years and has now returned to a Heritage Industrial location at Crossness. It is believed she was only saved at the Royal Arsenal because of "her name and humbling works the class had done to save the country" from possible enemy invasion. In 2000 she was sold to Waltham Abbey Royal Gunpowder Mills arriving at Waltham Abbey September 2000.

An artist's impression of the restored WOOLWICH.

Ian Bull, Precision Art

Returning to the present at Crossness, a journey on the new dual gauge line 18/24" being constructed, will start at the southern station located behind the Thames Water Pl., Inlet Pumping Station, and after small deviation to the east, follow alongside the recently built John Ridley Path, 700 metres to the northern station, sited just below the Beam Engine House.

As RANG (Royal Arsenal Narrow Gauge) established a base in 2016, in what was known as the ATCOST building it became obvious, as tracks were laid in the shed that awaited the dream to restore WOOLWICH was complicated by ownership issues and the major funds required to complete the works in a relatively short period of time. At a Trustee Board meeting in September 2017 the decision was taken and the current plans to adopt a dual gauge, 18"/24" not dissimilar to the old RAR. This choice afforded a wider range of narrow gauge stock availability and the future of visiting locos, also allowing WOOLWICH 18" metals to run on.

Crossness Pumping Station November 7th, Severn-Lamb locomotive BUSY BASIL, 2ft. gauge 0-4-0DH of 1986 arrived in the fading evening light, after a long haul from Haig Hall Miniature Railway at Wigan. Following on November 12th the first two carriages arrived. Enthusiasts note, this is the last remaining surviving "train set" built for the 1986 Great Stoke-on-Trent Garden Exhibition Railway. Opened by Queen Elizabeth II on May 1st 1986, it is highly likely that Her Majesty travelled in one of the compartments see photograph. RANG Railway will now build a dual gauge railway, on the old track bed of the original 1860 line from Plumstead station, with a target for completion of January 2019, subject to sufficient funding becoming available.

Built by Severn-Lamb Ltd., of Alcester near Birmingham in 1985 for the Stoke-on-Trent Exhibition, 1986 BUSY BASIL is the only surviving one of the four complete train sets that were built for this great celebration of modernity. This exhibition showcase to be the revival from the heavy industries of

Queen Elizabeth II in a Severn-Lamb carriage at the 1986 Stoke-on-Trent Garden Festival.

Author's Collection

steel and coal that had made men wealthy & devastated this area of Stoke for over 200 years. A narrow gauge railway (610 mm gauge) of nearly 4 miles length was built around the 180 acre festival grounds, having five stations located at key points, with an engine shed, located at the north end, that was reputed to have come from a disused British Steel shed left over before the site reclamation.

The four identical locomotives were all powered by Perkins 4236 diesel engines of 80hp. driving through a Linde Hydraulic transmission to all four wheels, with two independent hydraulic motors, one per axle and twin line air braking from the Perkins compressor. All the motive equipment for the Stoke project was just numbered unusually, 1 to 4, no Works No.'s were assigned by SL. It cannot be denied that whilst BUSYBASIL and her carriages are not "from that time" [ie. the 1920's] the overall outline, look and feel and character of the loco whilst not being "steam" is very much in keeping with the atmosphere one would want to generate on a site of the character and age of Crossness in earlier times.

Upon closure of the festival site, the entire railway was sold off, two sets went to the Bygone Village Museum in Fleggburgh, Norfolk, and the remaining were exported to an untraceable safari park in Spain. The locos plus four carriages retained for use at Fleggburgh. Sometime before this the locos received new steam-outline bodywork, work believed to be by Gentrac Systems Ltd and the carriages were rebuilt to be enclosed with full doors & windows, as opposed to their original "open style ". After 1998 at Bygone Village she (BUSY BASIL) was auctioned on site and whilst a timeline has been traced of recent history its authenticity is unclear, however she did surface at BeWILDerwood Adventure Park, Hoverton in Norfolk for a proposed 15" layout. (Never built) then lastly to Haig Hall at Wigan, Lancashire. As an interesting point, no one seems to know where or when then name BUSY BASIL was adopted, originally at Stoke-on-Trent she ran as "BANK OF SCOTLAND" No. 2 loco.

BUSY BASIL arriving at Crossness on 7th November 2017.

Simon Hodges

March 2018 - BUSY BASIL will run under her present name till 2019 as RANG Railway No.1 ready to leave the engine shed, surrounded by the crew of volunteers that have worked to so hard to bring her back to life and make this possible.

Whilst a great deal of the restoration work centred on the external corrosion of standing out for many years, replacing the buffer plates, cab steps remodelled smokebox door, it is believed she had not run for some 15 years at least before arriving at Crossness. Starting from the major overhaul of the wheelsets, bearings and triplex chains, followed a complete re-piping of the air brakes. The only major disaster was early in the project when the radiator core burst, which required a replacement and installation of efficient electric radiator fan. The electrical wiring loom was something of a nightmare, this loco did not come with a handbook and a set of drawings. As we progressed it became obvious that, when re-built to steam outline, the original loom was simply retained, just "stuffed" into the new body, with even the "windscreen washer" pump intact. All now runs well and restoration on the two carriages will commence by May.

RANG Railway needs your help and support please. Here is a unique opportunity to become involved in the first new build of a narrow gauge railway south of the Thames and within the M25 corridor for 80 years. A unique chance to support our cause and donate towards the £23,000 required for track material or the £19,500 for locomotive and carriage restoration, or maybe help as a volunteer. Be part of this exciting experience, bringing the first rail passenger service to Crossness, be stakeholders in this vital addition which could be the "Cathedral Express".

Parties donating could be eligible for Gift Aid increasing their donation by 25%. We are also in the process of setting up a Crowdfunding website to broaden our support base, where the monthly progress of track laying will be seen, with a video of track laying at Crossness.

Severn-Lamb BUSY BASIL can be seen on YouttTube working with carriages in 1998 - search Fleggburgh Bygone Village 1998.

See website Crossness.org.uk
Email to info@Crossness.org.uk
Or email parkinsonr@btinternet.com

BUSY BASIL with some of the restoration team at Crossness on 6th March 2018.

Author

CARRIAGES CAN BE INTERESTING!

by the Friends of the Thorpe LR

A modified Dunn carriage showing its yellow, red and blue colour scheme. The blue side board was a Watson modification to keep feet firmly in. Here it was being loaded for storage in Shildon, March 2012.
Philip Champion

Most people focus on the locomotive at the front of the train but they would be in a pickle without the carriages to ride in. Some interest is shown in them like the BR Mk Is and the Ffestiniog's vintage carriages. Going down the gauges, even minimum gauge and miniature carriages can be interesting as the stock which has run on one Teesdale line shows.

This line is 770 yards long, formed of two balloon loops with a slightly curved alignment between them. Built near the river opposite Whorlton village, four miles east of Barnard Castle in south County Durham, it ran commercially from 1971 to 2005 as

the Whorlton Lido Railway - one of several attractions at this long-established recreation site. It survived a plan to export it to Sierrra Leone and the current site owner allowed a Friends group to revive and run the railway now called the Thorpe Light Railway one Sunday a month from April to September.

Site operator Raymond Dunn had the original four carriages built to his

Four months after opening, one of the original Dunn carriages behind KING GEORGE. The raked-back look can be clearly seen as can the smart red and yellow paintwork.

Malcolm Paul

specification. Three were built for the opening with a fourth coming some time later. Components were ordered in and assembled on site. The chassis frames and L brackets came from British Steel in Consett whose manager Raymond knew. The bogies were bought in. A local Bishop Auckland company, identity not now known, built the wooden bodies. Assembly was by father and son Fred and Derek Wheatley, professional platelayers from east County Durham who had built the railway. The floor was quite high. There were six seats, all forward facing, for 12 passengers. Seats were made of two horizontal planks with a space between them and two almost vertical planks also with a space between them. The wooden side supports were raked back to give a classy look reminiscent of steamships. A low foot rail ran round the perimeter. On the

right i.e. non-platform side was a mid-level waist rail. At the front of each carriage was a metal bar to give some protection to the front row. Their suspension gave a smooth ride. Colours were yellow with red solebars and waistrail; paintwork was kept smart. Length was 164" over the dumb buffers and width 33¾" to 34".

The carriages were used a lot from the Easter 1971 opening: Sundays Easter to October, school holidays and any fine day in between. While four carriages were used when especially busy, often just three were used in the train. By summer 1972 a perspex screen was fitted to one carriage, now the front one, to protect passengers from smoke and dirt from Bassett-Lowke 'Atlantic' KING GEORGE. The same three carriages ran as a rake, with no swapping of vehicles; a fourth was added when very busy. Other engines to haul them were resident diesel WENDY, Bill Stewart's FLYING SCOTSMAN in 1976-79, Barnes 'Atlantic' JOHN and a Severn Lamb 'Rio Grande' diesel both in the 1980s. After 1988 the sole locomotive was WENDY. Another modification was putting horizontal

side boards on each side to prevent passengers putting their legs out after a girl badly gashed her leg when dangling it out as the train entered the station. Usually three carriages were kept in the tunnel with one left outside sheeted up for the winter.

At some point after the whole Whorlton site was sold in 1990 to the Watson family two of the carriages were extensively rebuilt to cope with a bodywork structural problem and to meet improved safety expectations. The WLR carriages over time had a problem with the seats moving when passengers sat against on them. (In fact the surviving intact Dunn carriage has a small L bracket fitted to one seat back and support to keep it more rigid.) This had been caused by dampness getting into the wooden floor so that the interface with the metal bolts was no longer tight and fully secure. The solution was to remove much of the two carriages from floor level and above. Six metal uprights - raked back in line with the other two carriages – were welded to the chassis frame. On the right side a long metal horizontal waistrail

Although looking worse for wear after a period of outside storage the two Watson rebuilds showing their metal body frame, red and blue colours plus closer-pitched seat planks.

Philip Champion

was welded to the top of these. A new floor and new wooden forward facing seats were fitted. Whereas the Dunn vehicles had space between the two boards for both the seat bases and backs the Watson seats had two boards for the bases with no space between them and one board for the backs. Presumably to improve safety, air brakes using car hydraulic fittings were fitted to the front bogie of both vehicles. High side boards running along above floor level limited the chance for passengers to dangle legs out. Safety chains were fitted to the uprights for each of the six seat bays on the left. The high waistrail on the right limited the chance to lean out on that side. Small hooks were fitted on each side of the chassis ends probably for safety chains as a back-up for the central

One of the two Dunn carriages rebuilt by Watson in the 1990s showing the original wooden seating but extra blue horizontal side boards fitted to keep feet in!

A modified Dunn carriage being loaded for storage in Shildon, March 2012.

A Watson rebuild just after unloading at Vintage Vehicles lorry museum (now closed) in Shildon for storage, March 2012. Behind it is the one intact modified Dunn carriage.
All: Philip Champion

One of the three ex-Ardmore Severn Lamb carriages being refurbished by the Bryants in Sheffield. They would arrive just a day or two before the railway reopened as the Thorpe Light Railway.

Jim Bryant

coupling bar and pin. The two rebuilds are slightly narrower and fractionally shorter: length 163¼" and width 31¾".

The other two, original Dunn carriages were modified by the Watsons. They had safety chains fitted between the wooden uprights on the left side. They also had side boards fitted to keep passengers' feet in; they would have to step over them at the station. One had the side boards painted red, the other blue.

A revised colour scheme came in. The two Watson rebuilds have a blue wooden lower rail on the left side which continues round the front, a red wooden rail in line with the centre of the seat backs and a blue metal rail on the right which is angled down in the first seating bay. Their blue and red colours matched the new colours of WENDY which had also had modifications. The four WLR carriages were used until the railway – and the Lido – closed on May 26th 2005. In that time they will have done countless circuits covering many thousands of miles. When the Friends revival began in 2012 three carriages were sent to covered storage at a Shildon lorry museum. When it closed a year later they were sent to open storage at Locomotion, Shildon.

In autumn 2017 three of them were transported to a Co. Durham industrial training centre where they will be rebuilt one at a time in the Whorlton style but with more safety features -continuing a tradition of improving these- including preventing passengers' feet from dangling outside. The third carriage will have an area for disabled passengers. When they return one by one they will form a 'heritage' set.

The fourth Whorlton carriage, one of the Dunn originals, was rather dilapidated but saw use in 2012/13 as the Friends began to revive the line. It was useful for carrying tools and as a platform for cutting overhanging branches. When riding it volunteers had to perch on the one horizontal plank left on each of the three seats remaining! The

A look at the four-bay open Severn Lamb ex-Ardmore carriage on a driver familiarisation run with 4wD BESSIE in 2015.

Philip Champion

vehicle was dismantled in 2014 and will be rebuilt as a works vehicle. Meanwhile one bogie from it was fitted with a floor initially to carry concrete blocks for rebuilding the station platform. Since then it has invaluable for works use whether hand-powered or hauled by 4wD BESSIE.

Though a trio of Severn Lamb carriages (along with their locomotive) were bought from the closed Lambton Pleasure Park Railway (formerly called Lambton Lion Park) in 1982 they were little used. This line was about 25 miles to the north east near Washington. From 1976 to 1982 they had run near exotic African and Asian animals. One station was Zoo Halt. A Severn Lamb 'Rio Grande' hauled them from near the bears, past the water fowl and to the jacob's sheep. These carriages had four seating bays with

pairs of facing seats for 16 passengers. Two were open and the third was roofed though that was not used at Whorlton and stood in the siding alongside the shed. Colours were black and brown. They were low for Whorlton's platform and one of the carriages had a tendency to derail. They were sold. The original 'Dunn' vehicles were the mainstay.

For the line's reopening in June 2013 Jim and Peter Bryant sent three Severn Lamb carriages on long-term loan. They were built in 1973 as a trainset for the 'Rio Grande' 2-8-0D which arrived here in 2016. They all worked at Leisureland Express in Galway then Perks Funfair, Ardmore in Ireland. They were certainly colourful, if not garish. Colours were: black frames and footwells; light body frame in green; yellow seats; red side panels and white fibreglass roofs. Jim bought them in 2009 and stored them for some months at the Windmill Farm Railway moving that November to the North Bay Railway, Scarborough still for storage.

The passengers' view from the Thorpe Light Railway's Severn Lamb train on the near loop between the shed and the station.

Philip Champion

In 2011 they moved to the Bryant's Sheffield workshop for restoration. Peter had a lot of rubbing down to do before painting. The footwells were removed, repainted black then reinserted. The owners found the fibreglass roofs "less than ideal". The vertical supports and roof were removed from one which is now an open carriage - and often the most popular particularly as it is usually next to the locomotive. With the other two Jim replaced the roofs. A wooden mockup was made for the new curved roof supports and the pieces were cut professionally. These were fitted then the roofs put on. Next they fitted the seat planking and varnished it. There are no side panels. Colours were more restrained with: black for the frames, footwells, metalwork for seats and roof frame; brown seats and light grey roofs. In fact, the colours are similar to the Severn Lamb set which worked at Whorlton in the 1980s. At Whorlton's high platform passengers again had to step down into them - and try to avoid hitting their heads on the roofs! This led to the top section of breeze blocks along the whole platform being removed in winter 2013/14. Now passengers can get in and out easier. These carriages are now the mainstay - ironic in view of the little use of the 1980s set. Each carriage has four seating bays with pairs of facing seats for 16 passengers though the end bay in one of the roofed vehicles marshalled at the rear of the set is reserved for the Guard.

These have been hauled by steam engines SMOKEY JOE, SOONY, EFFIE, Cagney 44, diesel BESSIE and normally run with the 'Rio Grande' diesel.

Who would have thought there would be so much variety and history in 11 carriages for a minimum gauge line?!

Above: A Severn Lamb ex-Ardmore roofed and open carriage as the Branch Line Society covering all of the outdoor track went onto the shed siding, December 2013.

Below: One of the ex-Ardmore Severn Lamb roofed carriages refurbished by the Bryants at the station during driver familiarisation with visiting No. 27 SOONY.

Both: Philip Champion

DIESEL DELIGHTS AT APEDALE

by Simon Lomax

Deutz 10050 and Alan Keef 46.
All photographs by the Author

Hopefully, most readers will be familiar with the Apedale Valley Light Railway – a 2'0" gauge line which opened in 2010. The railway was built and is operated by the volunteers of the Moseley Railway Trust. From the outset of opening to the public at Apedale, special events have played a key part in the annual calendar for the railway. This is the story of just one such event – the Diesel Delights weekend in October 2017.

Where did it begin? With 78 locomotives on site, the MRT collection at Apedale is one of the largest such collections in the UK. The vast majority of the fleet is non-steam – diesel, petrol and battery electric

(although a compressed air loco once visited for a weekend!). Most of these are operational – perhaps some better than others, but nonetheless operational. But the conundrum was that the useful work which many of these locomotives could actually do was limited. This is because, in line with modern safety requirements, the passenger train at Apedale is fitted with air braking, and so the hauling locomotive has to be similarly fitted. Anyone who has driven non-air braked passenger trains will attest to the feeling of reassurance which comes from having a powerful and reliable braking system available to the driver! All of the Apedale

Hunslet 1963.

steam locomotives are fitted with air braking equipment, but only two of the diesels – a Motor Rail and a large Baguley-Drewry – so only those locos could be normally used with the passenger train. Hence, most of the fleet was confined to demonstration freight trains, P-Way duties and occasional joyrides.

Inspiration from an answer came from our friends and fellow Staffordshire narrow-gaugers at the Amerton Railway. In 2015 and 2017, Apedale locos were invited to participate in diesel-centred events at Amerton. At Apedale, we have a very active group of younger members, and they were very much involved in the visits to Amerton – not least because in 2015, one of the locos which went to Amerton was a 1938-built Ruston and Hornsby named PLUTO for which the young members group had led the restoration project. After the Amerton trips, this group were very keen to arrange something similar at Apedale.

The young members group were tasked by the Trustees with making such an event happen at Apedale...the joys of delegation,

and the danger of making suggestions!

The clever chaps at Amerton had devised a means of temporarily equipping locos for air-brake operation. Simple – just copy that. Err, no, not that simple. There are no such things as common standards on narrow gauge railways, and each railway is responsible for the safety of its own operations. So, the engineers at Apedale developed a portable air-brake system, but very much inspired by the Amerton system. So, in the words of the Six Million Dollar Man "We Have the Technology".

In many ways, that's the easy bit sorted. Having an engineering solution to a problem doesn't make an event happen! Planning an event, especially for the first time, is very challenging. Let's have a look at the main areas of work.

Firstly, and foremost, safety. We want the event to be memorable, but for the right reasons. Making things safe is all about managing risk, and risk assessments are at the centre of this. Risk assessment is a concept which gets a bad press, but many

Hudswell Clarke D558.

people are alive (and intact) today who, in years gone by, would have been killed or maimed – just look at figures for (say) trackworkers killed and injured over the years. Also, it's a legal requirement – so there's no point arguing – just get on do it, and do it right.

Having decided how we can run the event safely, that leads to an outline plan of the event – what trains will we run, how often and crewed by whom? It should always be remembered that the overarching legislation for railways is the same, be it covering one of Virgin's Pendolinos at 125mph on a mainline or a 20hp Motor Rail at 5mph at Apedale. Seems a bit mad, but there's no point getting self-righteous about it, just accept the situation. One of the facets of this legislation is that anyone doing a safety-critical job needs to be trained and assessed for that job – and that particularly means drivers and guards.

Next, Money Matters. A small charity like the Moseley Railway Trust needs to keep a very close eye on the money, and events are always a challenge, because they are all about managing financial risk. Take too many risks, and have those risks go the wrong way and it's goodbye Trust and Apedale Valley Light Railway – not a difficult concept to grasp, but it's surprising how many struggle with the idea (ask the directors of Carillion if you don't believe me). Each and every decision has to be weighed using the likely cost and the likely benefit. For example, it would be fabulous to advertise our event on national TV during the middle of Coronation Street – but is that going to attract enough people who have suddenly discovered a long-suppressed desire to travel to Apedale? This is particularly difficult for a new event; keeping the enthusiasm of the organisers whilst having to temper some of the wilder plans with financial reality is a very fine line to tread. Also, one has to rely on judgement to forecast the likely numbers of visitors and hence the probable number of pound coins in the till at the end of the weekend.

Motor Rail 6035 on the Field Railway.

The two ex-Pilkington's Motor Rails, 11258 and 11142, also identified as 12 and 13 respectively.

Motor Rail 1369.

Lister 10805.

Having navigated this morass, why do we do events at Apedale? In some cases, it's a commercial motivation – family/kiddie focussed events do very well for a limited amount of effort. Events which attract the railway enthusiasts tend to be somewhat less satisfactory on the effort vs commercial payback chart BUT it's important to remember that everyone on the railway is giving their time voluntarily; part of the "bargain" is that people need to get enjoyment and satisfaction from their involvement, and events can be very motivating for the volunteer workforce. Also, it gets things done. Restorations and other projects need deadlines otherwise completion recedes into geological timescales. Having promised that such-and-such a loco, or bit of track, will be a vital ingredient of the next Diesel event is very effective at focussing minds!

Since this is an article for a narrow-gauge magazine, I'd better mention at least a little about the weekend and what happened. On each of the weekend days,

there was a vaguely-defined batting order of locos which would work a passenger train. They would be made operational in the yard area at Apedale. In some cases, this is a straightforward process, in other cases a certain level of persuasion can be needed. The running locos were then sent into the station loop in groups of three or four. After each loco had worked a turn on the passenger train, it would go to the back of the queue in the loop; once it was at the front of the queue again, it was time to swap the batch of locos for another group. We were fortunate to have three visiting locos, all from the West Lancashire Light Railway. A large 50hp Motor Rail (No.12, works number 11258 of 1964) was a twin of our own fleet No.13 (works number 11142), and also worked for Pilkington's Glass at their sand quarries in Lancashire. Getting these two to double-head a train was a key priority! A very original Petrol engine Lister (no.10805) was the second visitor. This was (until recently) the only Lister

A remarkable contraption - the "Panther Wagon", replicating a vehicle from the heyday of the Ffestiniog Railway's "Deviation".

with a 2-cylinder V-type JAP engine, and it worked at Springfield Tileworks, just a couple of miles from Apedale. There was an NGRS visit to this works in the 1970s, which produced many published photos of this loco along with an LBT-type Ruston, which is now preserved at Leighton Buzzard. The Lister attracted much admiration because it had the elusive "just come from industry" ambiance. The third visitor was a "Stand-up" Hunslet, works number 1963, which had a glamorous industrial career at Altham Sewage Works, Burnley. Thankfully, given where it worked, this loco did NOT have a "just come from industry" ambiance.

One further visitor should get an honourable mention; this was "The Panther Wagon" – essentially, a rail-mounted motorbike. This is a re-creation of something built in the 1960s to allow Ffestiniog Railway works to access their worksites on the Deviation. The Bolton schoolboys who built the original also built the re-creation – but they ain't schoolboys any more!

In addition to the locos running on the main line passenger trains, other were deployed on demonstration freight trains on the Field Railway. One of the great things about the Field Railway at Apedale is that we can run the more fragile locos away from the passenger railway, and hence not delay things too much when technical issues

arise – 70-year-old petrol locos can be a bit temperamental at times.

Saturday saw us run fifteen trains, with fourteen different locos in use. One train was double-headed, and one loco (ex Leighton Buzzard Motor Rail No.20 – works number 8748) proved particularly popular with a visiting group of enthusiasts and ended up working three trains. Sunday was a bit quieter – twelve trains were operated, and three "new" locos turned out. So, over the weekend, seventeen different locos worked trains.

Will we do it again? Yes, most certainly. Feedback from visitors was very positive, all our volunteers enjoyed it, and the Young Members organising group impressed everyone with what they had achieved. The dates for the 2018 diaries are October 7 & 8. But our main event at Apedale in 2018 is the third of the Tracks to the Trenches events. These events commemorate the First World War and the pivotal role which narrow gauge railways played in the "War to end Wars". Tracks to the Trenches 2018 is on July 13, 14 and 15 – keep an eye on the event webpage www.ww1-event.org or on Facebook for updates. More generally, the season at Apedale runs from Easter until the end of October – full details at www.avlr.org. uk.

UNUSUAL WORKINGS

Above: LYD and VALE OF FFESTINIOG approaching Rhyd Ddu from Caernarfon whilst deputising for a failed Garratt on 24th August 2017.

Richard Topham

Below: DIANA and LINDA 'top and tail' a Pont Croesor shuttle during the F&WHR's "Quirks and Curiosities II" Gala over the May Day Weekend.

Michael Chapman

ISBN 978-1-900340-4

NARROW GAUGE
NET
SUMMER SPECIAL

No. 3

£6.95

DONEGAL - HUNSLET 1215 - BURE VALLEY - HAY TOR
BAIE DE SOMME - SOUTHEND PIER - *and more!*

CONTENTS

Four Englands Then & Now   2

Donegal Today   6

Hunslet 1215, What Happened Next?   11

Overseas Interlude 1: Baie De Somme 2016   18

Bure Valley Railway, In The Beginning...   22

Narrow Gauge 2015   30

The World's Longest Pier Railway   36

Overseas Interlude 2: Bulgaria   42

Thorpe Light Railway: Plenty Of Progress   46

Hay Tor Hiking   50

Restoring A Rockershovel   56

Sepia Scenes   64

COVER PHOTOGRAPHS

FRONT: Hunslet TRANGKIL No. 4 in action at the Statfold Barn Railway's Autumn Open Day on 12th September 2015.

Keith Frewin

REAR: Talyllyn Railway No. 4 EDWARD THOMAS enters the loop at Abergynolwyn on 9th June 2015.

Peter Donovan

TITLE PAGE: A quintessentially English steamy summer's day scene on a private railway in Kent (further details not published at the request of the owner).

Keith Frewin

Published by Mainline & Maritime Ltd,
3 Broadleaze, Upper Seagry, near Chippenham, Wiltshire, SN15 5EY
www.mainlineandmaritime.co.uk - orders@mainlineandmaritime.co.uk - 01275 845012

Printed in Wales by Gomer Press,
Llandysul Enterprise Park, Llandysul. SA44 4JL
www.gomer.co.uk - 01559 362371

ISBN: 978-1-900340-36-6

NARROW G...
NET...

GW01081474

SUMMER SPECIAL

FOUR ENGLANDS
THEN & NOW

We begin this year's *Summer Special* with a look at the four 'Englands' on the FR, beginning on the facing page with PRINCESS, at Duffws c1939 (*FR Archive*) and King's Cross in February 2016 (*Chris Parry*). On this page we have THE PRINCE on the Cob in 1887 (*FR Archive*) and at Dduallt on 23rd May 2010 (*Andrew Thomas*).

WELSH PONY running round at Beddgelert on the Welsh Highland Railway in 1925 (*FR Archive*) and outside Boston Lodge following repainting on 1st May 2013 (*Andrew Thomas*).

PALMERSTON in service as a stationary boiler at Boston Lodge in 1950 (*FR Archive*) and lined up with its surviving sisters outside Boston Lodge on 1st May 2013 (*Andrew Thomas*).

DONEGAL TODAY
by Neil Tee

Away in the depths of County Donegal 100 years ago was a thriving narrow gauge system consisting of about 225 miles of 3 foot gauge track. As the 20th Century wore on, more and more traffic took to the roads and the two narrow gauge systems – The Londonderry & Lough Swilly Railway and the County Donegal Railway finally closed their rail operations in 1953 and 1959 respectively. Both companies carried on their road operations for some time, the County Donegal until 1971 when it was absorbed by CIE and the Swilly on its own, remarkably, until finally succumbing in 2015.

What remains of these operations has its greatest strength in nostalgic memories of the railway in the minds of the elderly of the

The sight that greets visitors to the Donegal Railway Heritage Centre, with a railcar trailer in the foreground, Coach 58 behind, and one of the 'red vans' adjacent to the station building.

All photographs by the Author unless otherwise credited

Donegal area and the railway enthusiasts who have studied the railway. In turn these memories were passed on to younger enthusiasts, both Irish and from further afield, and through their actions it is still possible to relive the years of the railways on Donegal. This is possible both through films that were, mercifully, taken at the time of operation and now available on DVD, and secondly by visiting the remnants of the railway operations themselves.

The longest established of these is the Donegal Railway Heritage Centre, which is installed in the old railway station in Donegal Town, and which for nearly 25 years has displayed to the public artefacts of the railway, photographs, story boards and items of actual rolling stock. The latter have been increased over the last few years as further items have been discovered, rescued and restored. These include the goods vehicles of the railway and the red vans that used to be towed behind the railcars, plus examples of the coaches and one of the railcar passenger trailers. The public are allowed access inside these vehicles, just as they were in the days of the railway, except that now instead of sitting down for a railway journey, they can see displays of the railway including working scale models, and the films mentioned above.

One of the most remarkable restorations is Coach 58 whose history goes back to 1879, with intermediate incarnations as one of the four most luxurious coaches on the Irish narrow gauge, to acting as a high class trailer for the Donegal Railcars and then to being cut in half after closure and becoming two holiday homes in different parts of Donegal. The two halves were miraculously found and have been brought back together and restored.

Also remarkable is the survival of the Donegal steam locos. One, class 5A, BLANCHE, is inside the Cultra museum, another, Class 5 COLUMBKILLE, inside the Foyle Valley Museum in Derry which is occasionally open to show other Donegal items. It is advisable to ring the Derry museum service if visiting in order to check. Another, Class 5, MEENGLAS, is in rather poor condition outside the Foyle Valley Museum. MEENGLAS and sister Class 5 engine DRUMBOE, sat at the site of Strabane station from the time of closure of the County Donegal until around 1987, when they were rescued and saved from oblivion by the combined efforts of the North West of Ireland Railway Society and Lord O'Neill of

One of the main attractions inside the Donegal station building is this scale model of the original.

Shanes Castle.

DRUMBOE was stored for a while in Stranorlar and then at the Donegal Railway Heritage Centre. In 2005 an Interreg IIIA grant was obtained for some €100,000 to be spent on arresting DRUMBOE's decline and performing significant restoration, to be done at the works of the RPSI in Whitehead, Antrim. DRUMBOE returned to Donegal Town briefly for a festival in 2007, now again able to be moved on her wheels but not yet able to steam. Again, almost miraculously after some 50 years in the open, professional inspection has shown that the boiler and firebox are repairable, so DRUMBOE is now some 60% restored awaiting funds for this work. A further engineering marvel is to be performed by the RPSI which will allow DRUMBOE to return to Donegal this spring looking complete for display, but actually without its boiler which will remain with the RPSI for repair. So, although only the models on show move at the Donegal Railway Heritage Centre, the displays will include a real and accessible original locomotive, coaches and goods vehicles, plus the

Top Half of coach 58 is collected from Muckish.

Centre Sadly the coach collapsed during its journey from Muckish to Donegal - this is the kit of parts that arrived.

Bottom The other half of coach 58 at Fintown.

The two halves pictured opposite were reunited and restored to their former glory, as can be seen from this view of the carriage body as it sits today, outside the Donegal Railway Heritage Centre.

displays, wallboard stories, artefacts and constantly playing DVDs in the old station house. Hot and cold drinks are available to help sustain you on a long visit.

Those who want to experience a real moving train on the old County Donegal have not been completely without option. Truly in the depths of the County well up Glen Finn, the Fintown Railway has operated the original County Donegal Railway Railcar No 18 along a three mile stretch of classic Donegal scenery alongside mountain and lough for the summer weeks and occasional other open days. The line goes from the original Fintown Station towards the original terminus of Glenties. The operation has experienced the usual

difficulty of persuading visitors to take the trip down Glen Finn to reach Fintown, no less a problem than that which closed the railway in 1952. When the train is running, however, this is an experience not to be missed.

So it is still possible to get a taste of the old County Donegal but you must prepare. While you can expect the Donegal Railway Heritage Centre to be open year round on weekdays, it is important to establish whether the other locations will be open on the days of a visit.

Contact information for the various locations is:
• Donegal Railway Heritage Centre, The Old Station House, Donegal Town. ++ 353 (0)74 9722655, donegalrailway@gmail.com, www.donegalrailway.com
• Fintown Railway, Fintown, Co Donegal, ++ 353 (0)74 9546280, www.antraen.com
• Foyle Valley Railway Museum, Foyle Road, Derry BT48 6SQ, Northern Ireland, ++ 44 (0)28 7126 5234.

The Fintown Railway. Simplex 102 is ready to depart with Railcar No 18. Used in push pull combination on an out and back journey, No 18 is an original CDR railcar from 1940.
Fionnbarr Kennedy

DRUMBOE in 2007, after completion of the Interreg financed partial restoration.

HUNSLET 1215, WHAT HAPPENED NEXT?
by Ian Hughes

At Apedale shortly after arrival.
Ian Hughes

My book, *Hunslet 1215, A War Veteran's Story* (published by Oakwood Press) told the story of Hunslet Engine Company works number 1215 of 1916 – a 60cm gauge 4-6-0T originally built to the specification and order of the British War Office for use on the Western Front – from 1916 up to it taking up residence at the Apedale Valley Railway of the Moseley Railway Trust (MRT) in 2008. This article hopes to give a general impression of the trials and tribulations in the subsequent 8 years.

For the next two years after arrival at Apedale efforts focused on fundraising and discussions with various bodies on how to obtain grants and gift aid. After receiving professional advice The War Office Locomotive Trust was formed and the locomotive's ownership was transferred

to it. This body was then able to become a registered charity and it also become registered for gift aid, both of which factors were a massive aid to successful fund raising. By 2011 enough funds had been accumulated to make a start with the initial target of the bogie and smokebox saddle casting. The latter was one of the biggest concerns as both "wings" had become cracked and partially broken by a combination of rust and the material that had been packed in around the live steam pipes. A start was made cleaning up some smaller bogie parts and also removing the 28 bolts that held the cylinders to the saddle through the frame.

It was quickly recognised that as the facilities at Apedale were still under development one option might be to see if the semi-independent team headed by Martyn Ashworth might be prepared to take on another challenge. They were restoring the MRT's own Hudswell Clark 1238 at a private workshop and there was likely to be a slight hiatus in 1238's restoration while more funds were assembled so this could work for all parties.

This was agreed by the WOLT trustees and the Workshop X team and so in February 2012 1215's boiler was removed (due to limited space at the workshop) and in April the rest of the loco was transferred.

The saddle casting - before and after.
Mike Lynskey

At Workshop X in April 2012.
Ian Hughes

The loco was rapidly dismantled to its component parts and the small items stored within the side tanks were all extracted and pored over. Approaches were made in various directions seeking assistance, which resulted in a generous offer from Graham Lee at the Statfold Barn Railway to overhaul the bogie for us to help get things moving. This left the team focused on extracting the saddle, which despite the previous removal of almost all the bolts still proved a challenge.

By November the casting was out and at the specialists and a quote for this and repair of a hairline crack in the left cylinder steam inlet port came to near £10k causing a sharp intake of breath. This just had to be held for further fundraising. Work continued on the frames cleaning, painting and examining. It was agreed to start refurbishing smaller items as funds allowed - first focus was the brake hanger brackets, frame stretchers (one was missing) and tank support

outriggers. Examination of the steam brake cylinder showed this to be in remarkably good condition.

Further assistance came again from Statfold with an offer to replace the driving axles (the originals had journals up to a ¼" undersize on diameter and needed further machining) and a full set of 4-6-0T drawings that they had in the Hunslet Archive. This revealed that of the six main axleboxes, only two were of original design – a one piece gunmetal casting. The others were in pairs, two made of cast-iron and two were fabrications.

The brake cross beams and pull rods were in very poor condition, however some were located from scrapped narrow gauge Hunslet diesel locos that could be modified to suit without too much effort.

The turn of the year to 2013 brought the extremely welcome news that an application to the Arts Council PRISM fund had been successful and the £20k this brought meant an immediate go-ahead on the saddle and cylinder repairs which were completed and returned in May. The decision was also taken to go ahead with a new set of axleboxes to ensure that everything was set up correctly at the bottom. The next bit of encouragement came in August with a donation of £5k and the potential of £5k more if we could match it by the end of November. This was helped along by a grant of £1.5k from the Transport Trust. Work progressed on reassembling the frames with a riveting campaign putting in 73 hot rivets using an enormous set of callipers and a hydraulic squeezer as a more neighbour friendly (i.e. quiet) means of carrying out this work.

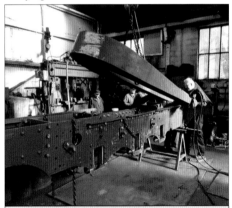

The giant callipers at work.

Mike Lynskey

With all this work in hand came the culmination of discussions with the Heritage Lottery Fund that had started in 2006 and finally concluded in November 2013 with a grant of £99,800 for the boiler. This was THE turning point for this project - now we felt that actually this will happen! This also had the knock on effect of boosting other support as it helped convince supporters that the project would be completed in a sensible timescale.

Off site at Statfold the news came that although the bogie was progressing, they were not happy with the condition of the bogie tyres. This was a bit of a blow and as it has turned out it was just one of quite a few to come as a result of a very hard 40 year working life then 27 years next to the sea. So we pulled the belt in and ordered some new ones. More evidence of its hard life came with the main springs - none were original, one was different from the rest and they all had one or two cracked leaves, so again new ones had to be ordered. The secondary suspension posed a particularly interesting challenge not least because the cylindrical rubber pads now had the consistency of coke, and the drawing only had the details for the compressed length.

Progress on the boiler started immediately. Prior to the HLF application various professional opinions had all come back with the same advice - that although the Bundaberg built 1940s vintage boiler was repairable, the same money would come close to purchasing a completely new one with a much better life expectancy. So a new set of drawings, based on the original design but to modern standard thicknesses was commissioned and approved, then a tender process initiated. At this stage we anticipated quite a tight timescale which limited our options on who was available. In February 2014 the order for a new boiler was duly placed.

Early 2014 also brought a slight change of plan. As previously noted 1215 was sharing the workshop with Hudswell Clark 1238 and this loco had a deadline of the September 2014 *Tracks to the Trenches* event at Apedale to meet. This meant 1238 needed all the attention of the volunteer team. In addition it had been found that the removal and refitting of many major frame components brought the release of some previously hidden "tensions" in the frame of 1215. These were probably from some heavy use and occasional derailments in its service life, which meant that they needed some serious attention to get everything straight and true again. So it was concluded that the frames were best temporarily transferred to a contractor's engineering workshop for setting up and they would also polish up the hornguides and match up the axleboxes to ensure everything was perfectly in line. Fortunately allowing a reasonable excess on the new axle box castings meant it was possible to grind back and polish the existing hornguides.

By September the Hudswell had been successfully steamed and commissioned and it was duly taken to Apedale to star at the planned WW1 event. With a pause for a couple of deep breaths the team swept the workshop and arranged for 1215's frames to return. The extra space also meant the tanks and cab could be more easily worked on. During the summer, the bogie had progressed well at Statfold with new tyres, bearings and axles fitted, only springs and hangers were outstanding, a new dome cover had appeared and the original safety valves had been dispatched for assessment.

With the focus back on 1215 and some funds in hand many parts started progressing, slide bars and valve spindles were ordered which unfortunately was also the case with the safety valves due to worn threads and hairline cracks. The frames were rubbed down and given further coats of paint, not without considerable debate on the exact shade to use on the inside, and the appearance of the re-gauged driving wheel sets back from Statfold was a major boost. The latter had not been straightforward - when re-gauged to 2'0" in 1924 Hunslet had fitted a new set of tyres with a thicker flange against the outside of the wheel centre. The tyres that were on 1215 were good enough to take a skim to the desired flange profile after the other work was completed. However, the lead two centres both had cracks so it was felt preferable not to reverse what Hunslet had done, but to leave the tyres in situ and move the centres on the new axles. The cracks were repaired but to minimise the stress on them the idea was to swap the lead and trailing wheelsets. A good idea but then that also needed a new set of crankpins. However, back at 60cm gauge means the wheel set back to back dimensions will now fit almost any nominal 2'0" gauge railway in the UK.

The wheelsets wait for an engine.
Mike Lynskey

Boiler progress was good with all the major components shaped and pressed during the year, and a start was made on assembly. Unfortunately the news came through that the contractor needed an extension on completion date at this stage due to external issues on another job having a knock on effect through the rest of their contracts.

The boiler shell arrives in November 2014.
Ian Hughes

With good progress having been made, 2014 ended with our benefactor producing another £1 for £1 offer up to £10,000.

Onwards in to 2015 which became a year of great progress but with plenty of knocks as well! The early part of the year brought the welcome news of the availability of a further four original Hunslet window frames and one or two other brass fittings which was a great relief. It also brought the news that grant applications to both the Foyle Foundation and The Garfield Weston Foundation had been successful, the first of the two was in time to help our many donors to reach the £10k target set in December. Unfortunately it was bad news from the boiler maker though, as four forged stays that we had planned to re-use off the old boiler could not be repaired to pass testing, and due to the limited number of locations that could carry out the work of forging new ones to the required standard it added an extra £5k to the boiler cost and a further delay. However through the summer the boiler did edge forwards though not at the pace we really needed.

The completion of the work on the main wheelsets meant that the axlebox journals could now finally be skimmed to size. This job was done and the magic day finally arrived when a wheelset could be refitted to the loco. Suspension parts were all being gathered and a methodology had been developed to produce the secondary suspension rubbers required. A sample of what we thought should be right was cast, then squeezed to the load as per the Hunslet drawing and a check made of the length. Despite being an educated guess with 100 year more modern materials it was right first

time. With the driving wheel sets ready, the almost complete bogie was returned from Statfold and the team finished off work on the hangers and springs, in order to complete assembly.

When initial restoration was commenced in Australia, nearly all of the bodywork was replaced as it was in extremely poor condition. Although the new items had been made to the Hunslet drawings they had all been welded. As our plan was to return to WW1 appearance some 450 hollow rivet heads were ordered, and using a series of accurately drilled jigs these were progressively welded on to the tanks and bunker by a very patient and skilled volunteer.

The hollow rivet heads welded to the tanks to recreate the original WW1 appearance.
Mike Lynskey

Effort also started to focus on the sanding gear, the only substantial part remaining being the boiler top pot for the front feeds which retained its seized mechanism. The two cab mounted rear ones were literally just a welded box with no holes in and a loose lid.

On the chassis the slidebars were very carefully set up and work on the slippers and crossheads got underway. Onwards through the summer more parts kept landing with a magnificent pair of safety valves delivered along with castings for the big ends, coupling rod lead end bearings, the refurbished valve yokes and guides being a few examples.

By year end all the brake gear was on site and ready to fit, consisting of new blocks and hangers, new pull rods, adapted

The completed bogie.
Mike Lynskey

The safety valves.
Mike Lynskey

Hunslet diesel crossbeams, new weighshaft with original arms, reconditioned steam brake cylinder and hand brake column. Taking stock towards the end of the year it was apparent that the poorer condition than anticipated of many parts had led to a drain on the Trust's finances and with grant options getting limited a discussion with our incredibly generous benefactor brought another matchfunding deal. This had the same format as before but this time the end was actually in sight and the remaining costs were quite clearly identified. The annual open day at the start of December brought the cheering sight of the boiler complete apart from dome, regulator and tubes. It was also evident though that with the boiler not yet complete, getting the loco completed and tested before the May 2016 *Tracks to the Trenches* event at Apedale was going to be a tall order and this would put unfair pressure on the volunteer team so we had to make the call in conjunction with MRT that we would have to cancel, much to everyone's disappointment.

And so into the New Year and the cloud that had landed with December's conclusion

lifted very rapidly as two years after the boiler had been ordered it finally arrived, and in a positive frenzy of work all sorts of things then suddenly came to completion. All the suspension went in for the final time, which meant the brake gear could be finished off, the tanks joined the bunker back in place, all of the newly created rear sanding gear was completed and pipes were running everywhere for lubrication and train braking systems. Suddenly 1215 was starting to look like a loco again!

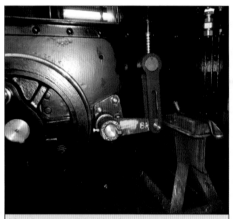

Newly assembled brake gear.
Mike Lynskey

New cladding has been made for the boiler, cylinders and brake cylinder, and the cylinder top sections proving particularly challenging. With the boiler on site work could progress with attaching the boiler fittings and crinolines. Early on the decision was made to retain the auto-positive injectors as fitted in Australia as this type is reliable and readily available, however whereas the Bundaberg boiler had external feed pipes toward the midpoint of the barrel, our new boiler was to the same basic design as the original. This meant creating from scratch a set of back head flanges and fittings complete with steam valve and clack, a task entrusted to the same gentleman who made the safety valves. If anyone needs to convert from Gresham and Craven No. 4 injectors then please get in touch! These fittings are very similar in appearance to the original fittings.

Pistons rods and rings have all arrived but there are still sections of the motion in progress or to order.

And this is where we are up to at the time of writing, it has all cost a huge amount more than originally anticpated which is frustrating as it was relatively complete, but as noted earlier the 40 years of a very hard working life added to 27 years in a playground near the sea all added up to a lot more work being required to ensure a safe and reliable locomotive for the future. All the removed parts have been retained as material record of the condition of 1215.

The final paragraph must go to the supporters without whose incredible patience and donations large and small we would not be so close to the finishing line, but we must also appeal to keep the funds coming in to complete the job properly in 1215's Centenary year.

If you wish to help or would like an update, visit our stall at Apedale or at Statfold or contact us via our website www.warofficehunslet.org.uk

The boiler backhead, showing progress on refitting components.

Mike Lynskey

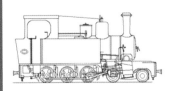

OVERSEAS INTERLUDE 1:
BAIE DE SOMME 2016
by Phil Barnes

The biannual(ish!) Festival of Steam at the Chemin de Fer de la Baie de Somme is a magnet for steam enthusiasts from all over Europe, and the 2016 edition was no exception. In this view, 2-6-0T No.15 of 1921 departs from a pathing stop at St Valery Canal, with the 13.00 Le Crotoy to Cayeux Sur Mer. The headboard is to mark 20 years of the twinning between the KESR and the CFBS.

All photos by the Author on 16th April 2016

2-6-0T No.1 of 1906 arrives at Noyelles with the 15.00 Le Crotoy to Cayeux Sur Mer.

Pinguely 0-6-0T no.101 of 1905 from the CFBS home fleet arrives at Noyelles, with the 16.00 Le Crotoy to Cayeux Sur Mer.

99 6001, visiting from the Harz departs Noyelles, with the 15.00 Le Crotoy to Cayeux Sur Mer after a loco change.

2-6-0T No.1 hauls the 15.00 Le Crotoy to Cayeux Sur Mer into Noyelles station prior to giving way to 99 6001 waiting in the foreground.The tracks behind the orange fencing are the SNCF standard gauge lines.

The diminutive 0-4-0T no.25 of 1927 departs Noyelles with the 14.05 Cayeux Sur Mer to Le Crotoy. Note the dual gauge track heading to St Valery on the right.

Visiting 0-6-0T loco J-S 909 of 1901 arrives at Noyelles with the 15.05 Cayeux Sur Mer to Le Crotoy on the 16-4-2016. This loco was visiting from the Blonay Chamby railway in Switzerland. The train is running over the dual gauge track to the main line.

BURE VALLEY RAILWAY, IN THE BEGINNING...
by Gerry Balding

The Bure Valley Railway is a 15" gauge line built on the trackbed of the former standard gauge Wroxham to County School branch. The line runs from the market town of Aylsham 9 miles to Wroxham which is the main centre of the holiday industry based around the Norfolk Broads.

The original standard gauge line opened in 1880 with passenger services being withdrawn in September 1952. In 1960 a curve was built at Thelmelthorpe to connect the branch with the last remaining stub of the Midland & Great Northern line to Norwich City for goods traffic. The last enthusiast specials ran in 1981 and the line was closed entirely the following year when the pre-cast concrete works at Lenwade (near Norwich) closed. In 1984 the track and ballast were removed.

The opening of the remodelled Wroxham station on 16th April 2016 brought the rare sight of three steam locomotives at the south end of the line. From left to right are 8 JOHN OF GAUNT, 1 WROXHAM BROAD and 7 SPITFIRE.

All photos by the Author

That appeared to be the end but the local authorities in the area were left with a network of rural trackbeds located to the North and East of Norwich. The question was what to do with them. A network of long distance rural footpaths was the answer.

Norfolk County Council and Broadland District Council jointly bought part of the trackbed from Hellesdon to Attlebridge. It was agreed that the County Council should acquire the section from Lenwade to

The author's first visit to the BVR was in August 1990, a few weeks after opening day, when visiting 4-8-2 SAMSON is seen coming off the turntable road at Aylsham. Note the original goods shed in the background, which was demolished the following year to make way for a sheltered housing complex.

Aylsham, whilst Broadland District Council would acquire the remainder from Aylsham to Wroxham.

At the same time Broadland District Council came up with the idea of a narrow gauge railway and took a lead role in developing the project. It purchased the trackbed, acted as agent for the railway company in progressing the necessary legal consents (including obtaining the Light Railway Order) and gaining the necessary planning permissions. Broadland also bought the former station and yard at Aylsham from British Rail to provide a station for the Railway and acquired sufficient land at Wroxham to provide a new terminus. The Council was also able to attract grants from the Department of the Environment and the

English Tourist Board towards the costs of the £2.5 million project.

Thus the inception of the Bure Valley Railway was different from other lines as it was not enthusiast led or backed by a wealthy individual.

The Council's partner in the venture was a Great Yarmouth based motor repair company Auto Plates who were backed by a local entertainments company, Pleasurewood Ltd, owners of the Pleasurewood Hills theme park near Lowestoft. John Edwards and Robert "Happy" Hudson, the owners of Auto Plates, had previously constructed a 7.25" gauge line at Pleasurewood Hills in 1982.

During the winter of 1988 Auto Plates built a diesel locomotive, wagons and a prototype coach in their yard at Great Yarmouth. The prototype coach is still in service today but is heavily modified as a generator car to provide electric train heating during colder weather. The diesel loco is still in service as BVR 3 2ND DIVISION USAAF hauling PW trains and passenger services when required.

Construction of the Bure Valley Railway began in May 1989 with the demolition of a store building at Aylsham by the late Fred Dibnah. The headquarters during this time were at Coltishall with work starting here first towards Aylsham. Construction of the line, including a new 200 yard tunnel under the Aylsham bypass, was completed in 364 days.

However it was not all plain sailing. Some residents at Buxton objected to the Railway due to the perceived negative impact on the quality of life in the village and the anticipated effects of increased tourism in the area. Interestingly the prospectus did not originally propose a halt at Buxton but included plans for a halt at Brampton and a passing loop and platform at Coltishall. Eventually the opposition at Buxton vanished and a halt was built on the site of the former LNER station (which still stands as a private residence). Since opening, the halt at Buxton has proved to be very popular and well used.

8 JOHN OF GAUNT passing the old Buxton Station building, now in use as a private residence, on 3rd August 2015 en route to Wroxham. The BVR's new platform is out of sight at the rear of the train.

The Railway was opened on 10th July 1990 by the late Miles Kington. The day was memorable, but almost for the wrong reasons. The first train hauled by SAMSON and WINSTON CHURCHILL (hired from the Romney, Hythe and Dymchurch Railway) carrying the dignitaries from Wroxham to Aylsham for the opening ceremony, experienced problems with the braking system. Accounts from the time describe how some of the guests had to get out and help push the train away from Wroxham. By the time the train arrived at Coltishall, it had failed and the diesel was sent to Coltishall to rescue the train. In the end, the train was over an hour late arriving at Aylsham. Hardly an auspicious start to life for the new Railway.

Despite the early optimism and enthusiasm, just six months later the survival of the Railway was at stake. In January 1991 the parent company (RKF Holdings of Pleasurewood went into receivership as a result of the property crash at that time. Receivers were called in to operate the Railway jointly with Broadland District Council until a buyer could be found.

It is fair to say that the Council held their nerve and continued support despite some stiff political opposition. To secure the future of the Railway the Council stepped in and bought the car parks and buildings at Wroxham and Coltishall to prevent it being sold for development. This ensured that the Railway remained as a complete entity.

There were a number of interested parties, but in April 1991 a new company, Bure Valley Railway (1991) Ltd, was set up to the buy the Railway. Thus the involvement of the original owners ceased and a new chapter opened in the Railway's brief history. Serious financial problems continued to threaten the existence of the BVR throughout its first decade. There were two further changes of owner after 1993 before the current not for profit company led by Andrew Barnes took over in 2000 and gave the Railway a secure basis for the future.

Looking back over the past 26 years, has the BVR been a success and achieved its

Top WINSTON CHURCHILL, one of the locos hired in from the RH&DR to operate the opening season, sits on shed at Aylsham in April 1991 shortly before returning home. Fellow RH&DR resident BLACK PRINCE can just be discerned behind.

Centre BVR 3 (at this point un-named) in its original dark blue livery as built. In April 1991 it is slowing for the road crossing at Belaugh Green with a train from Aylsham. The brightness of the headlights betrays the lateness of the hour... This loco was built by the original operators of the line and used on construction trains. It is still in service on the line today.

Bottom SYDNEY at Wroxham in April 1991. It is in 'as arrived' condition from Fairbourne.

aims?

The Railway now has a secure financial basis despite the scares and uncertainty of the period up to 2000. There were several occasions during that time when staff watched the last train of the season depart and wondered if this was to be the final train. The Railway survived these years due to the collective support and belief of the staff, volunteers and the Friends of the Bure Valley Railway.

The original prospectus for the company set out the aims of the project. It is interesting now to look back and to see to what extent these have been met. There were also some ideas expressed at the time which didn't come to light for one reason or another. There were four main goals for the project:-
•   To awaken a slumbering railway track;
•   To finance the creation and future maintenance of a long distance footpath;
•   To provide a further tourist attraction in Broadland; and
•   To bring benefits to the town of Aylsham

On 16th February 2016, 2-6-4 ZB tank 9 MARK TIMOTHY climbs Wroxham Bank with a "Teddy Bear Express". This loco, originally built to County Donegal outline, was rebuilt by Alan Keef n 2003.

(and villages along the route) through the generation of jobs and tourist expenditure.

The prospectus set out plans to construct and operate a 15" gauge steam railway between Aylsham and Wroxham which offered passengers the highest possible standard of service, comfort, safety and reliability. This has been clearly achieved. The Bure Valley is now a well-established heritage Railway and part of the 15" gauge community. During the first season (1990) the Railway carried 45,000 passengers. In 2015 this figure had risen to 116,126. From July 1990 to the end of 2015, a total of 2,634,147 passengers had travelled on the line. The adjacent footpath is well used by walkers and cyclists.

The Railway is an established part of the local community and tourist scene.

is not only an attraction in its own right but also links with other leisure providers. Boat trains are run from Aylsham with in conjunction with a local boat cruise company at Wroxham for which passengers can buy a combined ticket. The station at Aylsham has a successful café, souvenir and model railway shop which are open all year around even when trains are not running.

Originally an hourly service was proposed from both Aylsham and Wroxham for the peak season. The 1990 timetable allowed for a train every 68 minutes from 9.00am with eight trains in each direction. At that time the season just ran from July to October plus Santa Specials. In 1991 services started at Easter. In the 2016 peak season summer timetable, there are five steam and one diesel trains in each direction. The journey time has been slightly increased compared to 1990, a single journey now taking 45 minutes rather than the 40 minutes originally timetabled. This allows slightly more time at intermediate halts for passengers leaving and joining the train.

During the intervening years, the season has extended and now includes a number of popular events such as the Santa Specials, Teddy Bear Express and the Spooky Express aimed at attracting families. In 2016 the Railway runs daily from 19th March to 31st October. In addition out of season charter trains in January have proved successful in bringing visitors as part of a holiday tour package.

It was intended that the line would be steam operated from the outset first using locos hired from the RH&DR and then with its own motive power. For the first season SAMSON and WINSTON CHURCHILL were hired but returned home in March 1991 following the change of ownership. The new company obtained steam motive power in the form of SYDNEY (originally named SIÂN) and the SR&RL 24. These were attractive locomotives but not at all suited to the demands of the line. The situation did ease slightly after the steam outline diesel locomotive TRACY-JO was converted into the useful and popular steam locomotive WROXHAM BROAD. The Railway struggled in the early years for motive power until the first two ZBs (BVR 6 and 7) arrived in spring 1994 followed later by the two tank ZBs (BVR 8 JOHN OF GAUNT and BVR 9 MARK TIMOTHY) together with a Hudson-Hunlset shunting loco placed on long term loan to the company by the Friends.

The original plans were for a two train service with ten specially constructed coaches per train, carrying up to 200 passengers per trip. The twenty coaches were built but current train lengths vary depending on the passenger loadings and the season. Whilst ten coach trains are not unknown, they are the exception rather than the rule. The original coaches remain in traffic but have been modified and refurbished over the years. Four wheelchair accessible coaches were built in the late 1990s to supplement the fleet and provide operational flexibility.

The prospectus envisaged a workforce of 35 to run the peak summer service. The Council saw the project as a job creation programme in a rural area both during the construction period and afterwards. Although the local press reported in early 1990 that the Railway had given permanent jobs to 11 trainees (all of whom had been without work), what is not known is how many remained with the company once construction was complete. The Railway provides permanent and seasonal jobs in retail, catering, engineering and operations but not to the level anticipated. Perhaps the original target was a bit optimistic.

One proposal that did not materialise was the building of a diesel multiple unit to provide an all year round commuter service. During the operating season local people use the trains as a means of getting to Wroxham or Aylsham but the majority of passengers are visitors.

It will be interesting to see how the Railway measures up to its original aims and goals in another twenty five years. The Railway is not content with standing still. It is always looking for ways to improve facilities and the customer experience.

On 30th March 2016, 7 SPITFIRE runs alongside the River Bure near Hautbois Hall.

On the same day, 9 MARK TIMOTHY crosses the River Bure near Buxton.

On 22nd March 2016, 1 WROXHAM BROAD slows for the road crossing at Spratts Green.

On 30th March 2016, 9 MARK TIMOTHY pulls away from Buxton with a train for Wroxham.

Two photos from the Statfold Barn Railway's 6th June Open Day, (*above*) Corpet 439/1884 and HOWARD, and (*below*) vertical-boilered PADDY is in action on the Garden Railway.
Both: Peter Donovan

Four Quarry Hunslets form a procession up Ddolfawr Bank past Ddolfawr Crossing on the Bala Lake Railway on 31st August. Front to back: WINIFRED, ALICE, JACK LANE and MAID MARIAN.

IRISH MAIL and TRANGKIL No. 4 return to their birthplace at the site of the Hunslet Engine Company in Jack Lane, Hunslet, during the Middleton Railway's Hunslet 150th Anniversary celebrations on 18th July.

Both: Andrew Budd

The 2015 Gala at the Welshpool & Llanfair saw the visit of 0-4-4-0T PAKIS BARU No. 5 (O&K1473/1905) from the Statfold Barn Railway. It is blowing off nicely when pictured at Llanfair Caereinion on 5th September.

Keith Frewin

Meanwhile back at Statfold, resident FIJI (HC972/1912) is laying a fine smokescreen during the 6th June Open Day. This loco was returned to the UK in 2012, and restored in 2014, having previously been converted to a diesel loco on the island for which it is named.

Peter Donovan

Dromod station at the Cavan & Leitrim Railway, with signature loco DROMOD in light steam. Currently out of action the locomotive had a fire lit in the smokebox for the occasion. In the background is JOE ST LEDGER, a Ruston and Hornsby ex Bord na Mona loco.

Fionnbarr Kennedy

Kerr Stuart DIANA sits in the sun outside the Vale of Rheidol's workshops at Aberystwyth on 17th September. This loco is now based at the Bala Lake Railway.

Peter Donovan

2-6-2T LYDIA (AK77/2007) visiting from the Perrygrove Railway, having just arrived at Dalegarth with a nine coach service train from Ravenglass during the Ratty's Centenary of 15" Gauge Gala Weekend, 28th August.

Andrew Budd

27 SOONY in light steam at the Perrygrove Railway during their 19th September Gala Day.

Peter Donovan

THE WORLD'S LONGEST PIER RAILWAY
by Keith Frewin

Sir John Betjeman

In the early 19th century, Southend, like so many other seaside towns around the country, was growing as a holiday resort. It was particularly popular with Londoners who wanted the perceived health benefits of the seaside air. However, the coastline at Southend was predominantly mudflats, preventing the river and estuary steamers from berthing at the developing town. As a result, many potential visitors went further downstream to Margate, and other resorts where berthing was better.

To solve this problem, the first Southend Pier Act received Royal Assent in 1829,

SIR JOHN BETJEMAN heads away from the camera towards the Pier Head.
All photographs by the Author on 23rd June 2015.

and the first pier, a 600ft long wooden construction, was opened in June 1830. This short pier was still too short to be used by steamers at all states of the tide, and so the pier was progressively extended until by 1848 it was 7080ft long. The popularity of the wooden pier led to its ultimate demise, as its deteriorating condition led to its sale to the Southend Local Board (as local

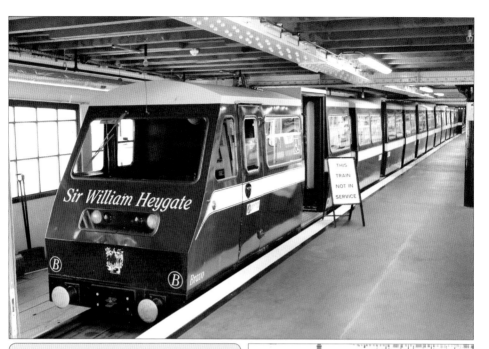

The journey along Southend Pier begins from the undercover Shore station. On the day of the author's visit, SIR WILLIAM HEYGATE was the out of service set (*above*), stored here so as to be available in case of need. The view (*right*) shows the approach to the station, complete with traffic cone blocking the "out of use" platform! The trio of pictures is completed (*below*) by an interior view of the pedestrian approach to the station - both trains can be seen in the platform, SIR WILLIAM HEYGATE out of service on the left, and SIR JOHN BETJEMAN awaiting passengers on the right.

government was then styled) in 1873. The Board decided to replace it with a new pier of iron construction in 1887. A horse drawn tramway was laid along the wooden pier in 1851, to convey passengers and luggage to the steamers.

The plans for the new pier included a 3ft 6in gauge electric railway. The railway started construction in 1888 and by 1890 0.75 miles (1.21 km) of single track was laid. The electrification of the line was carried out by Colonel R.E.B Crompton and a single toastrack style car was in use. The motor car was equipped with a 13hp motor taking a current of 200V DC. The current was produced from the pier's own generator which was belt driven from a Davey & Paxman 25hp steam engine. The line was extended to the full length of the pier and totalled 1.25 miles (2.01 km) in 1891, on completion trailer cars were introduced.

The infrastructure of the passing loop. Note the steel sleepered track laid directly on the wooden decking of the pier, and the colour light signal.

In 1899 the traffic on the pier had become so much greater that another two trains were required and a passing loop added. A second generator was also added but in 1902 Southend Corporation had established its own generating station and supplied the pier at 500V DC. This made the pier plant redundant and it was shortly after disposed of. With the new supply the motor cars had 18hp motors fitted to replace the old 13hp motors. The sets were also expanded, to four cars each.

In 1909 the four sets were equipped with a fifth car each. Unfortunately this made the power cars very much underpowered and so the five car sets where fitted with twin 27hp motors in 1910. In 1914 another eight cars where purchased making the trains up to seven cars each.

The conductor rail was replaced with a more substantial steel rail in 1911 followed by the running and conductor rails being replaced a few years later in 1919. In 1928 the passing loop was extended by 150 yards with work to double the full length of the running line taking place the following year, at a cost of £35,000.

A workshop was built at some stage on the west side of the shore under the station which handled maintenance requirements until 1978. This has now become the pier museum. A full signalling system was also put in with two boxes, one at each end of the pier. These both housed a seven lever frame and two 'Annett' keys. The levers consisted of 2 for the crossovers at each end, 2 home signal levers and 2 starter signal levers and 1 king lever which enabled the boxes to be switched out. The pier was closed to visitors during the Second World War, but (as HMS LEIGH) was used as an assembly point for convoys. The railway was used during this period to move casualties and ammunition from the ships to the shore.

In 1949 the four trains were replaced by four new seven car trains. These were built by AC Cars of Thames Ditton in Surrey and were finished in a green and cream livery. Each train could carry up to 260 passengers with a top speed of 18 mph. The journey took four minutes each way and trains ran every five minutes during peak times. The record for the number of passengers carried in one day stands at 55,000.

In 1950, two of the 1899 built trailer cars

Three views which illustrate the exposed nature of the Pier Head station, situated over 2km out into the Thames Estuary. As at the Shore station, there are two faces to the island platform, each dedicated for a specific unit.

The record-breaking length of Southend Pier is well illustrated in this view of SIR JOHN BETJEMAN approaching the Pier Head, with the adjacent walkway stretching into the distance, and the buildings on the seafront forming a distant skyline.

A final view of SIR JOHN BETJEMAN as it returns to the Shore station.

were sold to the Volk's Electric Railway in Brighton, where they were converted into motor cars 8 and 9. Upon their retirement in the 1990s, No. 9 stayed in Sussex, going to the South Downs Heritage Centre, but No. 8 returned home and is now part of the Pier Museum's collection.

By the seventies the traffic had slowed and the railway was only operating a two train service. One of the unused motor cars was turned into a permanent way loco with a flat bed - this was used as a works train and to carry goods to the stalls at the end of the pier. By the late seventies the pier was closed while extensive work was carried out, with the railway having been closed in 1978, and the trains scrapped in 1982. Examples of the 1949 stock survive in preservation in the Pier Museum, and at the Lynn Tait Gallery in Leigh-on-Sea.

Upon its reopening in 1986, the electric railway had been removed and a simplified 3' gauge track laid consisting of single track with a passing loop and two forks at each end for the stations. The service was operated by two seven car diesel hydraulic sets built by

Severn-Lamb. These were formally named by Princess Anne SIR JOHN BETJEMAN and SIR WILLIAM HEYGATE. A battery powered single car unit was introduced in 1995 to operate winter services. This is numbered 1835, the year that Southend Pier first appeared on the Admiralty Charts, and the year from which centenaries etc. are traditionally celebrated for the pier.

In 2006 the trains were repainted from their original burgundy with a white waist band into a two tone blue (but retaining the white waist band). They also now carry a Southend Borough Council logo. On 9th October 2005 the pier head got severely damaged in a fire where a pub a restaurant and the station was destroyed. The station was temporarily moved until a new modern structure was opened on the original site in September 2009.

The pier, still the longest pleasure pier in the world, opens daily from the beginning of April and runs trains on every hour and half hour from the shore end with two trains running a 15 minute interval service at peak times. There are no intermediate stations, the trains running non-stop to / from the Pier Head. The museum opens from early May.

OVERSEAS INTERLUDE 2: BULGARIA
by Ad van Sten

A steam tour operated on the 760mm gauge line from Septemvri to Razlog in Bulgaria on 11th and 12th April 2016.

Before WW II the Bulgarian Railways BDŽ ordered fifteen 2-10-2Ts from Schwartzkopf in Berlin for its 760mm lines. The design of this class 600.76 was based on the VIIK-locomotives in Saxony. Five of them, Nos. 601.76 - 605.76, were supplied in January 1941, but BDŽ had to wait for the other ten (606.76 - 615.76) until after the war. They came between December 1949 and March 1950; not from Germany, but this time from Fablok in Chrzanów in Poland. This second batch had two instead of four domes and the high smoke deflectors typical for Poland. They were the heaviest and strongest 760mm gauge locos in Bulgaria.

When the two main 760mm lines were dieselized, ten locomotives went to Cherven Briag for trains to Oriahovo. The other five stayed in Septemvri and Bansko as back up locos. Eight were scrapped in 1977 and another four somewhat later. The last ones were 603.76 in 1980 and 605.76 in 1983. Fortunately 609.76 (Fablok Chrzanów Nr. 1929/1949) and 613.76 were saved.

The c125km long line from Septemvri via Velingrad to Dobrinishte runs through the western part of the Rhodope Mountains. In particular the section between Cerna Mesta and Sweta Petka is spectacular. The line lost its freight traffic and there are only a very few passenger trains each day. We hope that you appreciate this collection of images which showcase the line at its best.

THORPE LIGHT RAILWAY: PLENTY OF PROGRESS
by the Friends of the Thorpe LR

The volunteers from the Friends of the Thorpe Light Railway were pleased at 2015's efforts and operations at this private Co. Durham 15" gauge line. Reinstating the tunnel roof was well under way, a new bridge had been built in-house, efforts to improve the trackwork backlog led to half of the 'straight' section (actually slightly curving) having fishplates and bolts removed, cleaned, greased and replaced as preparation for getting the track back to its original condition. Two public open days and two privately arranged days had gone well. On the public days replica

EFFIE's driver acknowledges the Guard's signal after the train clears the station points to head onto the straight section on July 26th 2015.
All photographs by Philip Champion

Heywood EFFIE visited from Cleethorpes to the delight of all. More progress could be made over the winter though Nature had some other ideas...

First, the running days. Diesel BESSIE did both private ones and the first trains in June's open day. EFFIE did familiarisation runs before the June open day with its minder from Cleethorpes and Thorpe's two passed steam drivers. Its strong whistle was its best advertisement. The next day a number of passengers from Whorlton village told us they knew steam was running as they could hear the whistle. July's running day was used for the annual barbecue which the site/railway owner has put on for Whorlton residents and the Friends ever since the line reopened in 2013. This gave us our best daily passenger total yet with EFFIE running 32 trains. After public trains, railway volunteers drove EFFIE under supervision as a training exercise. Just like replica Baldwin SOONY the year before it proved very responsive and a delight to drive. Standing in the 'well' also gave the driver very warm legs as the rest of the body cooled in the slipstream!

The wooden-sleepered bridge in the far loop carrying the line over the water channel as it swaps sides to go to the lake outflow pipe was replaced in house. Some of the sleepers were rotting through. The long retaining sleepers were dug out and new retaining walls built of stone. Girders were sourced and cut to size with two longitudinal ones positioned first then three transverse ones fitted above them to support the track. BESSIE and the 4w trolley made from one bogie of an original Whorlton Lido Railway coach proved invaluable in moving girders and stones plus taking old sleepers away.

One volunteer pointing the top row of breeze blocks on the tunnel south wall as another fills in the top of the blocks, April 2015.

By the time of the open days the tunnel walls in the far loop had been repaired and repointed. New doors were made then fitted. Part of the tunnel roof was restored to the delight of passengers young and not so young. In the autumn much of the roof was finished. Some concrete blocks had to be cut at an angle as the tunnel curves left twice in its 100 foot length. Invaluable again in moving bags of cement and sand to the worksite were BESSIE or the 4w trolley.

Work was programmed for the winter allowing for the weather, we thought. December 6th's working party could only observe Storm Desmond's damage and report back: the 'straight' flooded, a whole tree uprooted past the tunnel with its upper branches fouling the track plus a tree snapped over 30 feet up in the near loop before the curve back into the station. The next week's working party cleared branches from the water channels to help them shift the massive amount of water coming down the hillside which they were doing quite well. After two hours unpredicted heavy snow meant a quick exit for all. A visit a few weeks later found another tree snapped in the near loop just before the other one. Not only was the track flooded in the far loop curve

The new bridge in the far loop under construction, May 30th 2015.

Visiting EFFIE and train crossing the new bridge in the far loop.

been completely happy with vertical facings needing to be done and some flagstones uneven. An increase in volunteers has brought in more expertise. This February volunteers lifted and stacked the flagstones and cleared previous cement. With BESSIE bringing a roofed coach for clearances a start was made on cementing in a new course of breeze blocks. The 4w trolley was again useful for bringing the cement mix from the shed. In March cementing the blocks was finished with April planned for reinstating the flagstones.

Checking the new platform wall for clearance with one of the Severn Lamb roofed coaches on loan, February 13th 2016

but the lake overflowed onto it. The work programme was deferred as all efforts went on dealing with the weather's effects.

First, drainage channels were dug through the grass to let the water drain off the far loop curve into the adjacent field. Next one volunteer rodded the two lake outflow pipes to clear the blockage. The uprooted tree had its absolute myriad of smaller branches cut off then its trunk was cut up with the logs created stacked for local use. Work on cutting the two snapped trees in the near loop began in February with a winch later used to bring down the higher of the two. Clearing masses of leaves in the far loop cutting before the tunnel helped clear the track of water. A new ditch started in 2015 to bypass the lake inlet pipe which tended to clog up was proving successful and was widened, shifting the vast amounts of water into the lake.

Now back to some planned work. Three years ago the platform was lowered by one breeze block throughout to suit the lower Severn Lamb coaches on loan. We had never

For 2016 we have a lot to look forward to. Instead of two or three open days a year we are doing six: the third Sunday of each month from April to September. A Severn Lamb 'Rio Grande' should be on loan - the one which ran in Galway and Tramore with the coaches on site. Visiting steam is planned for some of the summer open days. Further details will appear on the Friends' website. Work on restoring original Whorlton diesel WENDY and the three Whorlton Lido Railway coaches should start offsite. The Friends are meeting with the owner of the railway and site to see how it can benefit local community groups as he wishes.

The aftermath of Storm Desmond - (*above*) an uprooted tree blocks the line on a partially flooded far loop; (*right*) two snapped trees foul the inner loop; (*below*) all are reduced to logs by the chainsaw!

HAY TOR HIKING
Narrow Gauge Railway Society

One of the many fascinating documents contained within the library of the Narrow Gauge Railway Society is a manuscript which records a 1930s hiking expedition along the remains of the Hay Tor Tramway on Dartmoor by one Victor M Falkner and his cousin, H John Falkner.

A first selection of these photographs appeared in Issue 235 of The Narrow Gauge, house magazine of the NGRS, along with a full history of the tramway. We are pleased to present here an extended selection of photographs, none of which have been previously published. The following is our hikers' description of the tramway:

"Runs from Hay Tor Quarries (Granite) to Stover Canal head at Lee Green in the parish of Teigngrace, Devon. It is fully delineated on the old OS 1809 revised circa 1835 maps. With sidings and branches at quarries it must have been well nigh 10 miles in length. The rails are of granite, average 4ft in length and about 10" x 20" in section with a flange worked in each length to a depth of 2" or 3". The rails are laid so as to give the standard axle gauge of 4ft 8" and with the flange inside a flat iron tyred wheel.

"The "points" for junctions are worked grooves in slabs of granite of sufficient size, with a wooden frog."

The remains of the track running from bottom right to top left in this view of No. 1 Quarry.

Above: The junction of the branches to Nos 1 & 2 Quarries, looking towards Bovey. The raised flange on the inside of the rails is clearly visible in this view.

Right: A close-up of the 'frog' at this junction.

Above: A number of these boulders were visible along the route. Presumably they had fallen from the wagons and were not worth the time and expense involved in recovery.

Below: At Lowerdown Cross, the trackbed (hand-marked on the print) runs alongside the road.

Two further views of the roadside section of line between Lowerdown Cross and Chapple Cross. In the view on the right, it can be noted that some of the "rails" have been moved to lie at right angles to the original formation - they now form the kerbstones for the driveway to Chapple House.

The trackbed crossing the Ashburton Road, 200 yards North of Pottery Cross, looking in the direction of the quarries.

The trackbed crossing the road from Pottery Bridge to Pottery Cross, again looking in the direction of the quarries.

Above: The overbridge at Ventiford, on the approaches to the canal basin.

Right: Journey's end, the basin at the head of the Stover Canal.

RESTORING A ROCKERSHOVEL
by Rob Needham

The oldest surviving Eimco rockershovel in the UK is this 12B at Dolaucothi.
All photographs by the Author unless otherwise credited

In May 2012 I was one of three cavers in the Forest of Dean who visited the gold mine at Lea Bailey and found that the lock on the mine doors had been broken and the doors were open. This was the first time any of us had seen in the mine. Several wagons were stored on the 2ft gauge track. And outside the mine the track curved away to the left, past an old tin shed. All looked derelict and abandoned. A more detailed history of the railway at Lea Bailey was included in *Summer Special No 2*; here is just a brief summary.

Having obtained agreement from the operators of Clearwell Caves, Ray and Jonathan Wright, who were also the operators of the gold mine, that I would

see whether a group of volunteers could be formed to revive the railway, in July 2012 work started to cut back the vegetation on the site. Then in September a shipping container was installed to function as a loco shed and workshop. Getting the Simplex loco working just required a new battery and some fuel, then it was moved from Clearwell to Lea Bailey. The Hunslet loco at Clearwell was a bit more challenging as it had an air starter, but we got it working by February 2013 and in April it was moved to Lea Bailey.

In the entrance passage at Clearwell

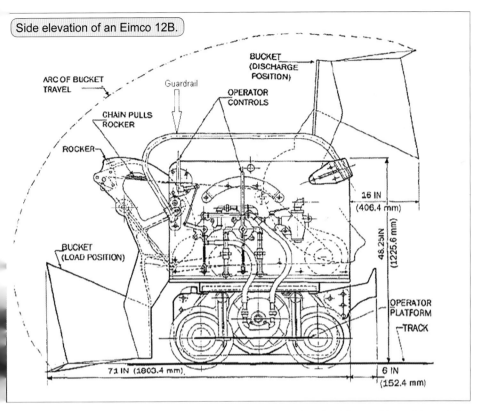

Side elevation of an Eimco 12B.

ARC OF BUCKET TRAVEL

CHAIN PULLS ROCKER

ROCKER

BUCKET (LOAD POSITION)

Guardrail

BUCKET (DISCHARGE POSITION)

OPERATOR CONTROLS

16 IN (406.4 mm)

48.25IN (1225.6 mm)

OPERATOR PLATFORM

TRACK

71 IN (1803.4 mm)

6 IN (152.4 mm)

were a WR5 battery loco and a red four-wheeled 'thing'. The WR5 was chosen as the next loco to get working, using four 12v auto batteries. By March 2013 it was working and then was used as a shunter at Clearwell for several months. However I was intrigued by the red 'thing', which was apparently an Eimco 12B rocker shovel. Which meant nothing to me. Ray Wright told me that it had been bought from the son of a miner in Devon. Following the death of the miner, his son had sold to Ray and Jonathan equipment that had been intended for a planned copper mine trial near South Molton. As well as the Eimco, the equipment had consisted of the WR5 and 6 Hudson U-tipper mine wagons

In the past I had seen rockershovels at various narrow gauge railway and mine sites – Morwelham in the early 1980s, Alan Keef's yard in 1995, Geevor in the 1990s before closure of the mine, Threlkeld in 2008. Having started work on the Eimco at Clearwell,

it was seeing the Eimco 21 working at the Apedale Heritage Centre that really fired up my enthusiasm to get the machine at Clearwell working. I was interested in finding out more about the Eimco and how to get it into working condition. Initial efforts were undertaken in almost complete ignorance. But as newsletter editor for the Northern Mine Research Society, an appeal in the August 2014 issue produced a copy of the Operators Instructions for the Eimco 12B and 21 (the 3¼ton 21 being the next size up from the 2 ton 12B).

The first stage in restoring it was to remove all the extraneous items that had been piled up on the Eimco. The two control levers were seized and immovable. So I decided to apply oil and then hit each of them with my trusty lump hammer. Slowly this treatment restored movement to the levers until both moved quite freely.

The bucket and rocker are held in place

Eimco B815 'as found' in passage at Clearwell, September 2013.

by four cables, two of 36" and two of 42¾" length inside the end fittings, but these had corroded so badly that two of the cables had disintegrated. The other two each remained in one piece, fortunately one of each length so I was able to measure the lengths. I was told that the Gloucester branch of Certex might be able to make up new cables, and a quick visit found one of their staff, David Clare, who had returned from retirement to help out with questions involving heritage equipment. He confirmed that the required cables could be produced – if I could supply new end fittings as Certex had nothing suitable in their catalogue. At the threaded

fitting on each cable, a spring was used to tension the cable. I was not able to find a source to supply new springs, so decided that I would use the old springs even though they had been somewhat damaged in removing the old cables and fittings.

To get new fittings made I went to see Tim Hodder, who ran an engineering workshop in nearby Whitecroft, to see if he could help. I left him a set of the end fittings from the old cables and a few weeks later a new set of fittings was ready for me to take to Certex.

I left the new fittings with David Clare, together with a note of the required cable lengths. And soon I got a call to say that the

Side view, showing control levers as found.

Set of new end fittings produced by Tim Hodder.

ables were ready for collection. Back at Clearwell, the next move was to try to get the rockershovel from the passage way to the workshop as it would be much easier to fit the new cables outdoors where there would be more space in which to work. This required it to be moved along the passage way for a few yards, then turned on a small wagon turntable, pushed out through the blacksmiths workshop, and then down the outside track, over a set of points, and back along the track to the workshop, where there was room for the Eimco to be stored under cover, although there was already an incomplete HC 0-4-0DMF stored in there.

The bucket drive chain, April 2014.

The rockershovel was on a short length of track (c6ft) in the passage way. A crowbar was used to inch the Eimco back and forwards on this short track until it was felt that movement was free enough to attempt the move to the workshop. With the clutch disengaged, the wheels were soon moving freely but as soon as the clutch was engaged the wheels locked, so it was obvious that either the transmission or the traction airmotor was seized. But at least with the clutch disengaged it was possible to move the rockershovel outside and down to the workshop (but carefully – as the only 'brake' was to engage the clutch!) Outside the workshop there was room to work on it and it could then be pushed into the workshop for protection when not being worked on. With the old springs, the new cables were fitted and the nuts tightened to tension all four cables equally.

The bucket is raised and lowered by a chain, driven via a pulley and geartrain by an Eimco 5-cylinder rotary air motor. But the chain had seized solid. To remove the chain, I liberally coated it with some old oil, then left it for a week or so before attacking it with the lump hammer. Once I had managed to get some movement in the chain, I then cut through the pin securing one end to the rocker. By this time I had made contact with Bob le Marchant, a contract miner/tunneller who had been involved in digging the tunnel on the Festiniog Deviation but who, more importantly, owned and operated an

Eimco 12B. He it was who explained how to disconnect the other end of the drive chain from the pulley which itself was driven by the air motor. Having removed the chain, I was then able to take it home to work on. It took repeated treatment with old oil, diesel, caustic soda, detergent and the lump hammer, but finally it was restored to near its original flexibility. To reattach it, I had to ask Tim Hodder to make a couple of steel pins to replace ones that had been cut in removing the chain.

With the chain reattached, it was obvious that the pulley itself or the drive from the airmotor was seized. Fortunately I found a large ring spanner at Clearwell that was just the right size to fit on the pulley lock nut. Then hitting the other end of the spanner with a sledge hammer eventually freed the pulley. This meant that the full drive from airmotor to bucket had been freed, but could not be tested until the rockershovel was ready to connect to an air compressor. But not yet.

At the end of July 2014, it became necessary to move the Hunslet loco back to Clearwell from Lea Bailey. To make room at Clearwell for the Hunslet, it was decided to move the WR5 and the Eimco to Lea Bailey.

With the Eimco at Lea Bailey, the next task was to get new lengths of air hose and use these to replace the perished hoses on the rockershovel. Then a first test with a compressor could be undertaken. It was only a small (14cfm) Draper compressor, way short of the 200cfm that the operator instructions said was necessary. But it was

Above: Unloading the Eimco at Lea Bailey, July 2014.

Below: Re-railing the Eimco, September 2014.

enough to test the operation of the bucket raising mechanism. Maybe only slowly, but the bucket was raised and lowered under control. So new cables, cleaned drive chain, new air hoses, freed controls, and airmotor all worked satisfactorily.

As a result we felt confident enough to hire a towed compressor and to operate the Eimco at our Open Day on 20th September (and found that 160cfm was adequate). The next day we hosted a visit by a group from Alan Keef, and found one problem in operating the Eimco. The broad wheel treads and thick flanges, while perfectly suited to operating underground on rough and temporary track, were not well matched with the Lea Bailey points. It derailed in front of our visitors. At least we had a willing and knowledgeable group to help re-rail it!

Buoyed up by the success of the open day, it was time to look at the traction airmotor. Bob le Marchant advised that removal was relatively straightforward, just a question of removing a few bolts. And so it proved. The problem was actually removing the motor. It was heavy - a three man lift where there was only space for two. Working in the open without any lifting equipment, we decided to tilt the Eimco over.

With the airmotor removed, it proved

Removing the airmotor while the Eimco is tilted to one side.

Freeing the airmotor.

simple to get it turning. Fortunately the $1/_2$" drive of a socket set fitted in the airmotor keyway. A sharp tap on the end of the toolbar and the motor was free to rotate. Then all it needed was a clean-up to remove the signs of rust where some water had collected with the oil in the motor. With the motor refitted and filled with fresh oil, as soon as the Eimco was connected to the Draper compressor the Eimco could be driven in either direction under control, albeit slowly due to the low power of the compressor.

Now we had a fully operational rockershovel ready for our next open day. But our Eimco was missing two items that would have been part of the unit when new. A guardrail and an operators platform (see drawing). Of surviving Eimco 12B rockershovels, only one appears to have kept the original guardrail and platform. That is the one at the Dolaucothi gold mine site in West Wales (this is apparently the oldest surviving Eimco rockershovel in the UK, US-built w/no 627 dating from c1940, formerly used in the Halkyn District United Mines in North Wales - now better known as the Milwr Tunnel, where there are still at least four Eimco 12Bs underground that are accessible by experienced cavers). So in July 2015, with a colleague from Lea Bailey, I paid a visit to Dolaucothi to measure the guardrail and platform to make patterns from

The new guardrail, made by Alan Keef, in position.

which replicas could be made.

Initially Tim Hodder attempted to bend a new guardrail from thin-wall steel tube, but found it impossible to achieve the required bends without the tube collapsing. So I asked Alan Keef if they could produce the required shape from thick-walled tube. As the photo shows, they came up trumps. All that was then needed was to weld a length of round bar in each end of the tube to enable the finished guardrail to be attached to the Eimco.

In October 2015 Bryan Lawson told me that he could get a new set of springs made for the bucket cables through Alan Keef. This enabled me to replace the original damaged springs that I had had to use when fitting the new bucket cables.

Finally, I asked Tim Hodder to produce

New set of springs with one of the damaged original springs.

a replica operator's platform. The original on the Dolaucothi Eimco was made up from two castings, but the new one would be fabricated. Unfortunately before it had been completed, Tim Hodder died in early March 2016. But his workshop business (Hodder Engineering) is being continued by Paul Callard who was keen to complete fabrication of the platform.

Then it will be ready to perform at the next Lea Bailey open weekend (in May), a fitting tribute to local engineer Tim Hodder.

Background

The Eimco 12B was a landmark in mining mechanisation. It is a compressed air powered, self-propelled mucker/loader and was the first machine to mechanise the loading of muck or ore into wagons at the rockface. Previously this task had to be undertaken by men with shovels, which was back-breaking work. It is usually known as a rockershovel because of the rocker on which the bucket was mounted. The 12B was designed in the 1930s and entered production in 1938. By the late 1960s nearly 30,000 had been made, and it was produced in several other countries as well as the US. From 1953 until 1978 the 12B and the 21 were produced in the UK by Logan Engineering in Dundee for Eimco (GB) Ltd of Gatshead. Some models are still in production in India and South Africa. The 12B at Lea Bailey has an Eimco (GB) plate with the number B815 stamped on it. This number is thought to indicate that the shovel is a post-1978 import, those produced by Logan having a four digit number prefixed LD.

There are about 60 rockershovels still surviving in the UK, although most are not in working order. Working rockershovels can be seen at Lea Bailey (May and September open days), Apedale Heritage Centre (Eimco 21, mining gala days), NCMME (Caphouse) (Eimco 21) and the Shropshire Mines Trust take an Eimco 12B to some shows. An Eimco 12B is under restoration at Geevor Tin Mine Museum.

Above: The rocker shovel, complete with operator platform mounted in position.

Below: An Eimco 12B in operation at Lea Bailey in May 2015 during a visit by the NGRS.

Bryan Lawson

SEPIA SCENES
Photographs by Peter Donovan

Sepia tinting has become unfashionable in recent years, however with the advent of digital photography it has never been easier to apply, and can give images an air of nostalgia which would otherwise be lacking. These two examples show DAVID LLOYD GEORGE at Tan-y-Bwlch and PRINCESS at Porthmadog, both taken in June 2015.